CW00448533

IN EXCITED TIMES

THE PEOPLE AGAINST
THE BLACKSHIRTS

NIGEL TODD

BEWICK PRESS / TYNE & WEAR ANTI-FASCIST ASSOCIATION

© 1995 Nigel Todd

First published in Great Britain by
Bewick Press   and   Tyne & Wear Anti-Fascist Association
132 Claremont Road   4 The Cloth Market
Whitley Bay   Newcastle upon Tyne
Tyne & Wear   NE1 1EA
NE26 3TX

ISBN 1–898880–0–1–8

Printed and bound in Great Britain by Trade Union Printing Services Ltd., 30 Lime Street, Byker, Newcastle upon Tyne, NE1 2PQ. Design, scanning and typesetting by Roger Booth Associates, Half Moon Chambers, 10 Bigg Market, Newcastle upon Tyne, NE1 1UW.

"So the evil moment of fascism came and was clear ... Since the actors cast to play the leading parts would not speak, the action was carried on by the peoples who used to walk to and fro at the back of the scene, softly laughing or softly weeping, or simply quietly being. Now these people streamed across the continents, inscribing their beliefs on the surface of the earth by the course of their flights, and on the sites of their martyrdoms. They defeated fascism by not being Fascist. They showed the contrast between fascism and non-fascism so clearly that the world, wishing to live, defended their side because it could be seen that they were the representatives of life."

Rebecca West, *The Meaning of Treason*, (1949)

ACKNOWLEDGEMENTS

A very large number of people have assisted with the research, discussion and publication of this book. Appreciation is due especially to members of the Tyne & Wear Anti-Fascist Association for their interest and encouragement, as well as to Raymond and Mabel Challinor and Archie Potts of the Bewick Press for their support and sharing of much useful historical information. Thanks are offered, also, to Francis Beckett for permission to read John Beckett's unpublished auto-biography, and to Polly Gorres of The Friends of the Chalet School for valuable insights into the work of Elinor Brent-Dyer. Much first-hand material was provided by Len Edmondson, Dave Atkinson, Frank Graham, Geoff Rossman, Richard Kelly, Tom Callaghan, Tom Hadaway and Irene McManus. As always, assistance was willingly extended by the staffs of the Newcastle upon Tyne, North Tyneside, Gateshead, South Tyneside, Sunderland and County Durham Local Studies Libraries, and their colleagues at the Tyne and Wear, Durham and Northumberland County Records Offices. The Public Records Office at Kew, the Wiener Library, the National Newspaper Library at Collindale, the National Museum of Labour History, the University of Newcastle Robinson Library and Durham University Library were extremely helpful, too. In addition, acknowledgement is made of kind advice received from Sir Jeremy Beecham, Councillor Teresa Russell, Keith Armstrong, Maureen Callcott, Lynne Otter, Ron Bill and Stan Newens, MEP.

This book would not have appeared but for the generous financial support of the Lipman Trust, the Barry Amiel and Norman Melburn Trust, the Paul Hamlyn Foundation, the Baring Foundation, David Gray & Company (Solicitors), Stephen Byers, MP (Wallsend), Nick Brown, MP (Newcastle upon Tyne East) and Bill Etherington, MP (Sunderland North).

CONTENTS:

ABBREVIATIONS

AFL   Anti-Fascist League (Tyneside)
BUF   British Union of Fascists (or, British Union)
CP   Communist Party of Great Britain
ILP   Independent Labour Party
MP   Member of Parliament
MI5   Military Intelligence (internal security service)
NUT   National Union of Teachers
NUWM   National Unemployed Workers' Movement
T&GWU   Transport & General Workers' Union
TUC   Trades Union Congress

ABOUT THIS BOOK

Most historians dream about finding a world frozen in time and hidden from memory. All you need is to find the key to some lost door and the dream will come true. For detectives of the historical persuasion, the keys to these discarded worlds rest in asking the right questions, and the questions are often prompted by a concern of the moment. *In Excited Times* had exactly these origins. When the Tyne & Wear Anti-Fascist Association was planning what became a huge carnival celebrating human diversity in 1993, someone asked casually if there was anything that could be included in the festival programme about earlier anti-fascist activities? A glance at the local newspapers for the 1930s revealed that there might be a great deal to be said about the efforts of a previous generation. The principal history books of the period, contrastingly, barely mentioned anti-fascism on the Tyne and the Wear.

Yet the question was the key. Once the question was put to those who lived through the 1930s, a flood of recollections and leads for further enquiries began to emerge. Posing the question in relation to the printed and written evidence of the time also pinpointed valuable information that had seemed of little consequence. Suddenly, a bunch of keys was to hand and the door was open!

The pathway to our anti-fascist past disclosed something that has been apparent for many years. Namely, that the beliefs and preoccupations of people who lived out their lives far from the centres of political power and media attention, who worked hard and depended upon their collective organisation and self-confidence to overcome the pressures of economic trauma, government indifference and war, nursed a treasure trove of real history. *In Excited Times* was nourished by the attainments of those men and women.

The past was a different place, of course. The Tyne and the Wear of the 1930s was a series of towns and communities linked with the vast expansion of heavy industry in shipbuilding, engineering, chemicals, coal-mining, steel production and armaments, as well as merchant shipping and fishing. A lot of this industrial structure was silent during the 'thirties, deadened by economic slump and government inactivity. As a result, widespread unemployment and grinding poverty afflicted colliery villages and towns such as Sunderland, Jarrow and North

Shields. People did what they could to fill in their days, and during good weather spent hours talking on the streets, a pastime that promoted not only gambling but also political meetings. Adversity encouraged a strong sense of community as another way of getting through the hard years.

Contrasts: Newcastle upon Tyne in 1935. Fell Street, Byker (above) and Market Street (below). Photos: Newcastle upon Tyne Dept of Environmental Health

But it was a changing world. The Tynesiders and Wearsiders of the 1930s enjoyed numerous cinemas, newspapers and magazines, dance halls, listened to the radio, and even television was in prospect at the very end of the decade. Traffic congestion on the streets of Newcastle upon Tyne and juvenile delinquency were seen as growing problems, while house building programmes by local councils and private builders were beginning to address a serious social shortcoming. Not everybody was out of work and some people clearly had money to spend on new consumer items.

The 'thirties could be very dispiriting. A "National", but really Tory, government held office, complacent about the condition of the country and serious problems elsewhere. Opposition parties looked enfeebled and in the doldrums. Meanwhile, laws restricting civil liberties were enacted. These ranged from the hated Means Test regulations of 1931, introducing state interference directly into the lives of the unemployed and their families, through the Incitement to Disaffection Act, 1934 and on to the 1936 Public Order Act, both severely restricting rights to hold public meetings and advance political opinions. A conservative bias in the administration of the state meant that these new powers bore more heavily against the Labour Movement and the Left. It was a trend that aroused suspicions of official sympathy towards Fascism, and prompted the formation of the National Council for Civil Liberties in 1934 to defend "the hard-won rights of citizens."

In the wider European world, considerable upheavals were underway, with Hitler's Nazi Germany and Mussolini's Fascist Italy offering their own solutions to the lack of employment. The violent rise of Fascism, first in Italy, then in Germany, spreading to Austria and later Spain, cast an anxious shadow. Newsreels and radio stations regularly broadcast the regimented imagery of Fascism, consigning creative human beings to ranks of marching, uniformed robots, dancing to the tune of strutting dictators bent on securing military might. By the end of the decade, war clouds were gathering.

This book looks at how working people on Tyneside and Wearside arranged a way of fighting Fascism, within a changing and worrying world. It was a Fascism that smashed forward across Europe and was delivered to British doorsteps by the notorious Blackshirts. For many anti-fascists, the Second World War started not in 1939 but in 1933 with

How Fascism Houses the Workers

Cartoon from the ILP newspaper New Leader

the rise of Hitler. And whilst it would be inaccurate to claim that anti-fascism was a prime concern of most people over the period – consistent activity was limited to a small minority of the population, and public expression of anti-fascism was the province of a larger minority – it was true that substantial numbers took up the Cause.

Is there any point to this kind of history? The story might be fascinating in itself, but does it have any wider relevance? Perhaps the answer comes back to the reason why this particular door to the past was opened in the first place. Once more, Fascism is virulent in Europe. From gangs of swastika-waving thugs, fire-bombing refugee hostels and black families, and on to political parties attracting millions of votes and even, as in Italy, joining the government, we again face the elements of a nightmare thought to be dead and buried half-a-century ago. So, how our predecessors dealt with a similar challenge is surely a matter of more than passing interest?

1: JURASSIC FASCISM

Our story begins with Alan Percy, 8th Duke of Northumberland. As one of the richest landowners in early 1920s England, the Duke was a deeply troubled man. From the ancestral home at Alnwick Castle, he surveyed a country disturbed by a recent world war in which victory had been bought at an immense cost in human lives and British power. And no sooner had the global war ended than the Irish, whom Percy regarded as "an inferior race", forcibly won a large measure of independence from the Crown. Irish nationalists in Dublin, the Duke fervently believed, would not be content until they had destroyed the British Empire.

Photo by   Lafayette.

THE DUKE OF NORTHUMBERLAND.

Over the horizon, a Red Revolution in Russia had abolished bankers and landlords and, nearer home, the Labour Movement was steadily gaining ground. Conceding no difference between Russian revolutionaries and Labour Members of Parliament, the Duke regarded the Labour Party as "merely the advance guard of Bolshevism" and traitorous "enemies of the social order." A "fanatic" in the judgement of even a sympathetic biographer, Percy was vehemently determined to protect his estates and wealth, and resolved on action. He therefore founded a newspaper, naming it *The Patriot*.[1]

The Fascisti

The Patriot was no roaring success but, in 1924, it carried the first notices announcing the formation of a Fascist party in Britain. These new Fascists, sharing the Duke's fevered anxieties, quickly attracted an array of middle class women and ex-army officers dedicated to upholding the Constitution, especially its least democratic elements such as the Monarchy and House of Lords. To cultivate an *esprit de corps*, the British Fascisti Ltd, as the party was called, promoted its own "Fascist label" cigarettes, matches, neckties and, for officers only, car-bonnet pennants!

There was a more sinister side to the Fascisti. Across the country, they established a para-military type of organisation under the authority of "Zone" and "Area" commanders. A Newcastle upon Tyne branch was opened in April 1925, operating from 148 Barras Bridge under "Zone Commander" Major R. Ewart Cree. Gripped by rabid anti-semitism, the Newcastle Fascists saw "international Jewry as the source of Bolshevik conspiracy", and set off to extend their network to South Shields, Seaham, Durham, and Whitley Bay.

Amid a flurry of whist drives and dinner dances, a Sunderland branch was started at 11 Norfolk Street controlled by 'Area Commander' Captain T. Thorburn Nesbitt. This proved to be a mistake. Nesbitt disliked the Italian-sounding name of Fascisti (the party's founders warmly admired Mussolini and his blackshirted cut-throats) and disruptively campaigned for a new title. In part, Nesbitt was motivated by rivalry with the breakaway "National Fascisti" which had formed a group in Newcastle. The National Fascisti's vicious members actually wore black shirts, distinguishing themselves from the British Fascisti's army surplus bits and pieces (a uniform known as "Black and Tan" previously issued by the British colonial authorities at Dublin to mercenaries in 1920). Mutual acrimony soon reigned throughout the movement, locally and nationally.

Apparently, British Fascism was falling apart almost at inception. Despite a vain attempt at overcoming splits, mounted by the British Fascisti's leader Brigadier-General R.B.D. Blakeney, who held rallies at Newcastle's Conservative Club and the Northumberland Hussars Drill Hall in October 1925, the entire North East organisation had collapsed by May 1926. The final whimper was sounded by Major Cree, the "late Zone Commander", urging such itinerant Fascists as remained to become strikebreakers during the 1926 General Strike.[2]

Shortlived and semi-comical as the British Fascisti's presence on the Tyne and the Wear may appear, it foretold several fault-lines of a native

Fascism: preservation of private property rights, a preoccupation with the officer-class, gross self-importance and reciprocal jealousy, a willingness to engage in para-military violence and, underpinning all of these, racial and political hatreds. These ideas could be found throughout the British Right in the inter-war decades, but Fascists took them to nightmarish proportions.

1931 And After

Elsewhere in the undergrowth, different ambitions were stirring. In 1931, the minority Labour Government led by Ramsay MacDonald, the MP for Seaham Harbour, collapsed in the teeth of an international financial crisis. MacDonald took a few of his Labour colleagues into a "National" Government of Tories and Liberals, devastated the Labour Party at a frenzied general election and then embarked upon drastic public spending cuts, wage reductions and mass unemployment. The number of people out of work nationally reached almost three million in January 1932, and a punitive "Means Test" withdrew unemployment relief from hundreds of thousands and lowered benefit rates for millions. Not surprisingly, the industrial areas were swept by serious clashes between the police and the protesting unemployed, as at North Shields in the autumn of 1932.

The impact of MacDonald's "betrayal" on the Labour Movement was far-reaching. Trade union strength was severely weakened. Within the Labour Party, divisions over policy exploded, and the left-wing Independent Labour Party walked out of the Labour organisation. There remained behind a lengthy running battle between a lacklustre, uninspiring Labour leadership pitched against the Socialist League, a campaigning pressure group supported by many of the Party's radical constituency activists. Labour's electoral recovery in the 'thirties proved slow and the "National", but really Tory, Government was again returned to power with a large majority at the 1935 general election.

The 1931 catastrophe also "laid the seeds of the birth of fascism" in Britain according to Len Edmondson, a Gateshead ILP activist in his youth. Certainly, the crisis posed an opportunity for a wealthy, disaffected ex-Tory, then Labour politician named Sir Oswald Mosley. Alienated from the conservative policies of the MacDonald

Unemployed workers lobby the Trade Union Congress at Newcastle upon Tyne, September 1932.

Government, and annoyed by his inability to secure high office, Mosley created a 'New Party', advocating increased public spending as a solution to economic slump. Mosley and other New Party hopefuls contested the 1931 general election, though with little effect.

One New Party candidate was Stuart Barr, a former Labour Party organiser who had spent part of the 1920s in North Shields lecturing on Socialism. Having fought Tynemouth, unsuccessfully, as a Labour parliamentary candidate in both 1924 and 1929, Barr was recruited to the New Party by Mosley. Barr stood for Gateshead in 1931, scoring only 1077 votes after a heated campaign made rougher by a Labour awareness that Mosley was heading in the direction of Fascism. Not everyone who joined the New Party became a Fascist, and numbers soon deserted in alarm at Mosley's contempt for working-class voters. But following a visit to Mussolini in Italy, Mosley finally converted the New Party into the British Union of Fascists in October 1932.

The British Union Of Fascists

The British Union of Fascists absorbed, too, the remnants of the British Fascisti. Consequently, aspects of 1920s fascism became embedded in the BUF. They were congealed in a bizarre marriage of reaction and "revolution" with Mosley's economic nationalism, embracing trade protection and state controls. Unlike the concept of Socialist economic planning, matching production to meet social needs, and based upon public ownership, parliamentary democracy and independent trade unions and co-operatives, Mosley sought a "Corporate State". This Fascist apparatus was to be run by a Leader (or 'Caesar-man') assisted by a national assembly selected from major corporations and tame Fascist-operated labour syndicates. The model for the BUF was Mussolini's Italy – both Mosley's new Fascists and the previous generation could agree on that position – but there was a developing interest in the Nazi "revolution" that overwhelmed Germany in 1932–33.[3]

For Italian Socialists and other democrats, Fascism had meant no liberty, prison and murder; for German democracy, trade unions and Jews and other minorities, Nazi rule installed murder and concentration camps. But in the trauma of post-1931 Britain, Mosley's BUF unveiled for many people a deceptively simple route out of chaos, a clean break with old failures.

Oswald Mosley: All dressed up and with somewhere to go? Photo: Newcastle Chronicle &
Journal

2: OFFENDING AGAINST COMMON DECENCY

Since 1882 Newcastle upon Tyne's Town Moor has hosted a great annual fair for a week at the end of June. Now "the Hoppings", the festival was generally known by its old sporting name of Race Week during the 1930s. Attracting tens of thousands of Tynesiders, Race Week was a landmark in popular entertainment, and an "oratory meeting" held immediately prior to the fair gave all manner of political and religious speakers a chance to engage with lively audiences. Race Week 1933, however, was destined to be different. Mosley's men had a scheme.

Following the formation of the BUF, Mosley quickly picked up recruits in Newcastle and its adjacent districts. William Joseph Leaper, for example, was a journalist on the Newcastle *Evening Chronicle*. A former active member of the Independent Labour Party in Yorkshire, he was a New Party candidate at Shipley in the 1931 general election. Embittered by MacDonald's premiership, Leaper joined Mosley in the BUF in the autumn of 1932. The Fascists also enrolled a Newcastle print worker, W. Risden, another ex-ILP man. Risden and Leaper at once started a BUF branch in Newcastle and, quietly but surely building a group, they plotted a way of bringing Fascism to public attention.

Learning from a rather inglorious first appearence for Fascists in the North East – a street meeting by two Blackshirts (Mosley put his followers into black shirts as uniforms) outside Sunderland Boiler-makers' Hall on 16 March 1933, ending when a crowd chased them away – Leaper and Risden moved carefully. On 15 June 1933, with Race Week in sight, the Newcastle BUF suddenly held an open-air propaganda meeting at the town's Marlborough Crescent bus station, where the speaker was accompanied by about 30 well-dressed men. Having declared their presence, the Fascists felt sufficiently bold to intervene at the Race Week speakers' corner on 18 June. Accordingly, five Blackshirts arrived with a lorry for a platform and opened their meeting. The result was not quite what Leaper and Risden had planned. The crowd noticed that the Fascist speaker "bore a striking resemblance to Herr Hitler" and reacted by overturning the lorry and hounding the Blackshirts "continually."[4]

Social Solidarity

What caused the reaction of the Town Moor audience? Communists were blamed for the disruption, yet their attitude at this time was a good deal more restrained. They had actually prevented a woman from physically assaulting the Blackshirts at Sunderland, and the Communist Party's Tyneside district committee had agreed to debate with the Fascists at the Newcastle Debating Society. This was in line with the current international Communist policy of regarding Fascists as no different from any other "bourgeois" party (a view soon to change).

The roots of the Race Week opposition to the Blackshirts rested in the culture of the Tyne and the Wear which grated against the bigotry of Fascism. Historically, the area had absorbed waves of immigrants with very few severe outbreaks of ill-feeling. Irish, Scots, West Indians, Italians, Poles, Africans, Eastern European Jews and Yemeni Arabs, attracted to the North East by the expanding industries and mercantile trades of the 19th and early 20th centuries – and, occasionally, warmly welcomed as political refugees – had produced a high degree of tolerance. As if to underline the continuing vitality of internationalist concerns, Newcastle had staged an enormous public meeting at the City Hall in May 1933, called by 130 political, industrial and religious leaders, to condemn Nazi anti-semitism in Germany. Sunderland also held a large meeting.

Added to the relatively cosmopolitan outlook, there was another local tradition crucial in understanding working class opinions. Towns and villages clustered along the two rivers had bred strong organisations in the form of trade unions and co-operative societies, not to mention the myriad of religious chapels and recreational clubs. The occupations of these communities, such as coal mining, ship building, seafaring, and engineering, generated a keen sense of solidarity since mutual support was vital to survival. Out of this social structure had emerged a radical political strain dating back in virtually an unbroken line to the 1820s.

Campaigns for social improvement and political rights often aroused enthusiasm, and by the early 1930s (despite the MacDonald debacle), a powerful Labour Party position was being established on the Tyne and the Wear together with a small but active Communist Party. The Independent Labour Party maintained a virile organisation boasting

70–100 members in Gateshead in 1933, a further 90 in Newcastle East (where a Socialist Cafe offered a focus), Guild of Youth groups and some 27 other North East Party branches. Already, in April 1933, the North East ILP was arranging for delegates to attend an Anti-Fascist Congress at Paris, and in May the Party helped to convene a meeting of 60 trade union and Socialist delegates "to discuss the Fascist menace to working class organisations and ideals." The conference voted to set up a North East Anti-Fascist Committee. An anti-fascist Workers' Rights Committee was also sponsored by the ILP in Gateshead.

Unfortunately for the Fascists Leaper and Risden, their Race Week appearance coincided with Hitler's ruthless suppression of German trade unions, co-operatives and left-wing political parties. It was hardly surprising, therefore, if the Town Moor crowd drew their own conclusions. In the words of the anti-fascist, Len Edmondson, the Fascists "offended against the common values of decency" that held together the organisations, traditions and communities of the area.

Fascist Terror

Common decency, of course, did not worry Leaper and Risden. After all, millions of Italians and Germans had held "the common values of decency" but this had not stopped Nazi and Fascist movements from winning power. The BUF set out with a similar dedication to purpose. Socialist League meetings were attacked by Fascists at Chester-le-Street and Durham in August 1933, and about this time the Newcastle Blackshirts confirmed the creation of a "corps" of young men "taught boxing and physical training" to assist the BUF. A Fascist Society was started in late-1933 among students at Newcastle's Armstrong College (the forerunner of the modern University of Newcastle), and the College magazine, *The Northerner,* was soon recording the wrecking of a Socialist Society meeting and a debate. The property of Labour-controlled municipal councils and Labour Parties at Blaydon and Sunderland were damaged by Fascists under the pretext of raising Union Jacks on "Red" buildings.[5]

Behind the wave of intimidation, the Fascists embarked upon a crusade aimed directly against the Labour Movement. A BUF office was opened at 129 Adelaide Terrace, Benwell, to strike at the heart of what the

The Fascist Society

Our Society, though but in its infancy, is definitely flourishing and we are now an approved College organisation; our Constitution having been passed by the S.R.C. at their January meeting.

Our aims are to study up that interesting movement in political thought, namely Fascism, and especially as it may affect Britain. Every undergrad. ought to have some knowledge of the various political thought, and we hope that, by our meetings, some clearer insight into Fascism may be obtaine...

Our last meeting, at which Mr. Alexander Raven Thomson spoke, was a great success, and those present are to be congratulated for the interest evinced. Possibly, our next meeting will be held at the beginning of next term. We expect to have a speaker equally as good as those whom we have had. All College students are welcome to our meetings.

T. E. CLEUCH BATTY, Hon. Sec.

Student Nazis: Armstrong College, Newcastle, students' magazine, The Northerner, March 1934

Fascists regarded as the "Red district" of West Newcastle, and steps were taken to organise the unemployed in a campaign against the Labour council at Washington. Infiltration of the bus workers' branches of the Transport & General Workers' Union at Chester-le-Street and Newcastle was attempted, and the recruitment of disaffected Socialists including Alec Miles, active in the Gateshead ILP's Guild of Youth, was achieved.

The initial success of the BUF should not be overstated. Although shocked, the Labour Movement did react. The CP cancelled their debate with the BUF, believing that "the mass opposition of Tyneside workers" on the Town Moor now made debate "unnecessary." T&GWU officials acted to stamp-out Fascist intrusions at bus depots "by holding meetings at the affected places", exposing and isolating the perpetrators. Meanwhile, opposition to Blackshirt meetings on the streets was clearly evident. "Several hundreds" of people, singing "The Red Flag" chased the Fascist speaker Captain Vincent Collier and his "defence corps" out of Sunderland town centre on 19 September 1933, eventually besieging Collier inside the railway station where he was protected by the police and an exceptionally large Blackshirt (nicknamed "King Kong" by the anti-fascists!).

A few days later, the luckless Collier found his speakers' rostrum overturned by 500 anti-fascists in Newcastle's Bigg Market. Back in Sunderland, a United Front Committee, created by the ILP, CP and the National Unemployed Workers' Movement, was planning an anti-fascist demonstration for October. Dismissing hostility from the Labour Party's leaders, who opposed any joint work with the Communists, numbers of Sunderland's Labour councillors backed the United Front departure.

BUF Advance

None of this stopped the BUF. Amply backed by the *Daily Mail* and Italian money, Mosley had the resources to expand his party at a spectacular pace. The autumn of 1933 saw a surge in BUF membership numbers and local branches in Northern England and Scotland. Large offices and clubs were opened at Newcastle and Durham. At one point, the BUF was negotiating with Newcastle Corporation to lease an old police station on Westgate Hill (the property was valued at £30,000, a tremendous sum in 1933 prices) for use as a headquarters. The Newcastle BUF, acting as a regional organising base, moved into 2 Clayton Street in the town centre in December, taking over two floors encompassing a club-room and office suites.

From small beginnings, the Blackshirts claimed to have built a membership of "hundreds" and 14 branches by the close of 1933. As a Newcastle Liberal, J. Howard Black, told the Sunderland Women Liberals that the rapid rise of the BUF had "altered the political landscape", a jubilant Mosley arrived in Durham for a rally of his North East legion. Leaper, Risden and Alec Miles, in the meantime, had gone to full-time jobs with Mosley in London, promoted for their services.[6]

Union Jack Curtains: Durham BUF office, Claypath, Durham, 1933–34. Photo: Durham University Library

THE POLITICS OF ANTI-FASCISM: A GUIDE

The Labour Party

The Labour Party (f.1900) is a federation of trade unions, local Labour Parties, Labour Women's Sections, Co-operative and Socialist Societies. Its aim in the 1930s was the extension of public ownership of industry and finance and planning of the economy enabling full employment and social reforms to be introduced. Labour, as a democratic Party, was committed to achieving its Socialism by winning elections and enacting the necessary legislation through Parliament. By 1932 the Party had over 371,000 individual members, and had formed two governments, 1924 and 1929–31, despite having a minority of Members of Parliament. Labour MPs numbered 287 in 1929, dropped to only 46 in 1931 but rose again to 154 in 1935. Between six and eight million people voted Labour by the 1930s, and the Party had begun to establish a strong position in local government, notably in industrial areas like County Durham.

Fierce debates on how to respond to Fascism were a feature of Labour's annual policy-making conference. The Party's leadership, supported by the main trade union leaders, usually won the conference votes, insisting that public condemnation of Fascism and support for refugees from Fascist regimes should be combined with opposition to direct action against British Fascists. Labour leaders argued that street confrontations drew attention to the Blackshirts, produced unnecessary violence and allowed Communists scope for extending their influence. The fear of Communist growth resulted in Labour Party members, including the Party's future leader, Hugh Gaitskell, being banned from speaking on anti-fascist platforms that included Communists.

The Labour Party often assisted humanitarian appeals for refugees from Fascism. In 1937, the Party's new leader, Clement Attlee, visited the International Brigade engaged against the Fascists in the Spanish Civil War and allowed his name to be adopted by one of the Brigade's fighting units. However, Labour's official anti-fascism remained fairly passive. This did not prevent several trade unions,

Labour MPs and scores of Party members from actively taking part in all manner of anti-fascist campaigns.

The Independent Labour Party

The ILP (f.1893) helped to form the Labour Party. It had explicitly Socialist aims and, through its own annual conference, local branches and MPs (37 by 1929), the ILP pressed Labour to go further and faster in implementing a Socialist programme. The Party was deeply opposed to Ramsay MacDonald's public spending cuts in 1931, and the following year the ILP left the Labour Party altogether. By severing the link with Labour, the ILP went into rapid decline. Membership fell from 17,000 in 1932 to 4,400 by 1935 when, at the general election, the number of ILP MPs was reduced to four, all from Glasgow. Clydeside and the North East of England remained as relatively strong centres of ILP support during the 1930s.

The ILP sought a new role as a democratic Socialist party but embracing, too, a strand of revolutionary Socialism encouraging direct action. In this context, the Party stood between the cautious, parliamentary stance of Labour and the militant ambitions of the Communist Party. ILP-ers were to the fore in taking direct action against Fascists both in Britain and in Spain during the Civil War (1936–39). The Party also urged a "United Front", intended to bring together all sections of the Labour Movement including the Labour and the Communist Parties in a common struggle against Fascism. At the same time, most ILP members and leaders remained critical of the Communist Party, and especially of the latter's willingness to accept Moscow's bloody executions of other Communists. The ILP clashed bitterly with the CP over the conduct of the Spanish War.

The Communist Party Of Great Britain

The CP (f.1920) brought together several left-wing groups in order to promote Communism as expressed through the Russian Revolution of October 1917. The Party sought a revolutionary workers' overthrow of capitalism and was intimately linked with the Russian Communists through the Communist International. The Party could claim to be part of a growing international movement of world revolution, but its political position was laid down by Moscow through the International. This placed the British CP in difficult situations.

Fierce antagonism towards "reformist" labour parties prevented united opposition to the rise of the Nazis in Germany and, although this line was dropped after 1933 in favour of "United Fronts" with democratic Socialists, the CP could never gain acceptance by the Labour Party's leadership. The CP's initial support for the Second World War against the Nazis, its sudden opposition to the War on orders from Moscow, and then its total involvement in the war effort following the Nazi invasion of the Soviet Union in 1941, again illustrated the Party's difficulty.

The Party did win substantial sympathy and thousands of members during the 1930s by its resolute opposition to Fascism on the streets of British cities and the sacrifices of its members on Spanish battlefields. Anti-fascist activity in Britain owed much to the unstinting work of Communists, though anti-fascism was by no means an exclusively Communist preserve. The CP also enjoyed a body of support in working-class districts, enabling the election of a Communist MP for West Fife in 1935 as well as numerous councillors, including a number in the mining areas of Northumberland and Durham. CP national membership stood at about 6,000 in the early 1930s and rose to over 12,000 by the middle of the decade, reaching 17,000 by the outbreak of war.

The Socialist League

The Socialist League (f.1932) acted as a pressure group within the Labour Party. Formed by left-wing Socialists who declined to follow the ILP "into the wilderness", the League spent much time seeking to win support at Labour conferences for radical Socialist policies. League members, who numbered no more than 3,000, tried to persuade local Labour Parties to elect left-wingers to the Party's governing committees.

The League was very active on Tyneside and took part in anti-fascism. Often acting as a bridge between Labour Party members and ILP-ers, the League favoured "United Fronts" against Fascism. This proved too much for the Labour leadership and, when the League issued a "Unity Manifesto" with the ILP and the CP in 1937, members of the League were threatened with expulsion from the Labour Party. The League therefore dissolved itself in May 1937. Undaunted, the anti-fascism of ex-League members continued and in 1939 they again tried to promote a "Popular Front". Those responsible, including some future Labour Cabinet Ministers such as Stafford Cripps and Aneurin Bevan, were temporarily thrown out of the Labour Party.

Among those expelled was Sir Charles Trevelyan, a radical Liberal turned left-wing Socialist who had been a Labour MP for Newcastle upon Tyne Central until 1931. Coming from a long-established Northumberland family of wealthy radicals, Trevelyan had been a Labour Minister for Education, and from 1930 he acted as Lord Lieutenant of Northumberland. Having a left-wing Socialist and anti-fascist as the King's official representative in the county was a source of gratification for the Northumberland miners, who regularly invited "Good Old Charlie" to speak at their Annual Picnic (or gala). Rejecting the concept of inherited wealth, Trevelyan left the family's stately home, Wallington Hall, to the National Trust when he died in 1958.

Sir Charles Trevelyan speaking at an International Brigade Memorial Meeting in Newcastle City Hall, 15 January, 1939. Photo: Frank Graham

3: THE FRIENDS OF BERLIN

Tom Hadaway, the Tyneside playwright, has a vivid memory of the 1930s:

"I imagine there was some kind of conspiratorial structure of Fascist sympathisers in the NE, and winning the war probably stopped them coming out of the woodwork, but this is just one anecdotal hint ...

I started working life, fifteen years of age, in a shipbroker's office in Milburn House, Newcastle on Tyne. Paid two pound a calendar month by a boss who was into the coal trade as a broker. He was shipping 1,500 tons of Ashington steam coal on a weekly packet from Blyth to Hamburg. Nice little earner for him, and it was going to go on forever. The receiver was Krupp Rederei und Kohlenhandl, which was the Essen gun makers coal and shipping company in Hamburg. He used to go to Hamburg, and attend the rallies, and come back telling us what a great thing work and discipline were. He definitely thought the Nazis were alright."

After war broke out, the shipbroker "was getting ready to hang himself from a lamp post" because hostilities had interrupted German payment for two shiploads of coal. But he need not have worried:

"Seven weeks after war was declared, all that outstanding money came to him by Bill of Exchange from Kleinworts Bank, Amsterdam. They paid the bugga off. They had no need to. Britain was impounding German assets, and taking German cargoes as contrabrand in the blockade. But they saw their mate alright. Speaks for itself! I reckon he had his swastika armband in the closet."[7]

Tom Hadaway's reference to a "structure" of Nazi sympathisers poses the question of the extent to which Fascism exercised an appeal outwith the committed membership of the BUF? At a national level, Mosley was receiving substantial support in late-1933 from figures such as Lord Rothermere, owner of the *Daily Mail.* The former Liberal Prime Minister, Lloyd George, regarded Mosley as "a very able man" and doing "no harm", and there were many others in the top echelons of

English society who more or less encouraged Fascism for diverse reasons. In the North East, Fascist or Nazi connections were detectable as well among the political and business elite.[8]

German Consul

A pivotal element in Tom Hadaway's "structure" was undoubtedly the German consular office at Newcastle. This was directed by R.H. Hopps of Harper, Hopps & Co., Shipbrokers, at 25 Queen Street, on the city's Quayside. Hopps acted as the Nazis' diplomatic representative throughout the 1930s and was assiduous on their behalf. Early in 1934, Hopps was busily persuading the Newcastle watch committee to censor a film entitled *Whither Germany?* The film was vigorously denounced as "frankly anti-Nazi propaganda and clever propaganda at that" by Mosley's newspaper *Fascist Week*. Composed of right-wing councillors, the watch committee leaned towards Hopps's representations, which were backed by a German Nazi, F.K. Neukirch, living at Ryton. The film was eventually shown at Newcastle's Haymarket Cinema but, under pressure, the cinema manager "deleted certain matters from the preliminary announcements", appeasing Hopps and the watch committee.[9]

Hopps did not go unchallenged. At the beginning of 1934 he was confronted with a deputation organised by the Socialist League protesting at the political repression in Germany. The deputation probably made little impact since Hopps and his family were well on their way into the Nazi fold. During the following October, the consul's daughter, Marie Hopps, a drama lecturer at Newcastle's Municipal College of Commerce, went public on a series of visits she had made to Germany. Euphoric at photographing Hitler, she confirmed her intention "to convince her English acquaintances that Hitler is not the ogre that some people believe him to be." She insisted that the Nazi leader would "justify" the faith placed in him, and brushed aside recent political executions in Germany as "a regrettable necessity". It seems fair to assume that the German consular office was not simply a conventional diplomatic and business arrangement but served as an arm of the Nazis in the North East.[10]

Mussolini's Man

A similar function was performed by the Italian vice-consul in Newcastle, Signor N. Tognoli, representing the large Italian community resident in the North East over many decades. Close relationships had existed between Italians and North Easterners and, in the previous century, huge public meetings had raised money for Garibaldi's campaigns to liberate Italy from foreign rule. Numbers of Tynesiders had also gone to Italy in a volunteer British Legion to fight alongside Garibaldi in 1860. Tognoli, seeing his task as one of promoting Fascism to English audiences, accepted speaking engagements and at first found an interested response from church and other groups. Mussolini's portrait was even mounted alongside that of King George VI in Newcastle's eighteenth-century Assembly Rooms, a favourite venue for "society" social functions.

Italian Fascists salute the War Memorial, Eldon Square, Newcastle upon Tyne, June 1934. Photo: Newcastle Chronicle & Journal

The vice-consul was employed, too, in assisting Fascist penetration of the Italian community. Young Italians were offered a chance to attend Fascist summer camps in Italy, and Fascist clubs were opened for adults in the North East. By 1939, most local Italians were included on Fascist membership lists (with or without their knowledge) held in Italian businessmen's offices at Newcastle and Middlesbrough. The eventual outcome was sad and deadly. When war came, the police seized the membership lists and used them to intern many innocent people. Some of the internees then lost their lives when the Nazis torpedoed *The Arandora Star* transporting them to camps in Canada. Fascism therefore soured previously good community relations and, as always, brought grief and death to those whom it touched.

The Fascist Society

Owing to the proximity of the exams., it was decided not to hold any open meetings this term, but we hope to entertain several prominent Fascist speakers next year.

An interesting invitation to be their guests for a fortnight has been extended to the Society by the Nazi students of the University of Marburg; it may be possible for some of our members to accept this invitation.

I expect the Society to carry on even more strongly next year, and to keep up a lively interest in Fascism, at the same time upholding in the College true spirit of loyalty and patriotism.

T. E. CLEUCH BATTY, Hon. Sec.

Today the Exams, Tomorrow the Reich! The Northerner, June 1934

The presence of consular offices formed an important link in the Fascist propaganda machine on Tyneside. And the existence of Fascist states offered opportunities for entertaining potential English converts. The Armstrong College magazine, *The Northerner*, for instance, carried an advertisement in 1935 inviting students to join a German Academic Bureau "educational trip", including sightseeing and lectures on Nazi economics.[11]

Rotary And Fascism

These kinds of exchanges also featured in the programme of the area's Rotary Club movement. Rotarians were usually business or professional people meeting regularly for lectures, social events and extensive charitable work. Rotary generally aimed its recruitment at the middle class, seeking out men who were relatively influential in the civic or business worlds or beginning to advance their careers. It was an elitist exercise combining local branches with an international organisation. David Shelley Nicholl, a prominent British Rotarian, noted with anger in his history of the movement, *The Golden Wheel*, the extent to which Rotary's international outlook was permeated by Fascist sympathies for much of the 1930s. But it was not just at the international level of Rotary that the Nazis found receptive minds. Tyneside Rotarians also harboured their share of enthusiasts for the new order.

George W. Idle was a schoolmaster and, in the early 1930s, the membership registrar of the Newcastle Rotary Club. Germany was one of Idle's passions and, in June 1933, he addressed the Darlington Rotarians on "Germany Today", having recently returned from a German holiday. Conferring approval on Nazism, Idle argued that Germany was now "more united" and "more peaceful" and the Germans were "more contented" under Hitler, who enjoyed support from "90 per cent of the whole nation." Rotary Clubs, said Idle, should work "on similar lines" to Hitler and Mussolini and "train the youth" for "peace." Although rejecting the Nazi boycott of Jewish businesses as a "mistake", Idle accepted that the rough treatment of the Nazis' Jewish and political opponents, and even the suicides among the Nazis' potential victims, were simply unavoidable by-products of the "revolution."

By coincidence, German Rotarians were present at a Rotary conference in Durham and this contact with an increasingly Nazi-dominated section of the movement was warmly cultivated. Another party of German Rotarians, led by the Nazi Karl Schippert, attended a further Rotary function at Durham in September 1933, and joined the Blackshirts in returning Fascist salutes in the city's streets. This strand of Rotarianism continued unchecked on Tyneside well into the middle of the decade. George Idle went on arranging Anglo-German visits and youth exchanges, and could be found organising "a big party" of Newcastle Rotarians to visit Hamburg in May 1936. The Newcastle manufacturer, Ernest Weeks, the managing director of Weeks, White & Co., which traded extensively with the Nazis, represented the Newcastle Rotary Club at a Rotary International conference at Hanover in June 1934. On his return to Tyneside, Weeks told the local press that the notorious Nazi Brownshirt thugs were "an inspired movement, rather akin to our British Legion."[12]

Hitler's Admirers

There is little to suggest that the BUF gained organisationally from the wider interest in Fascism. The Blackshirts, unconvincingly, claimed support from "many Newcastle businessmen" in June 1934, and a Labour Party survey that summer revealed only "an odd Borough Councillor or past Borough Councillor" had joined the BUF in Durham City, and had "endeavoured to get recruits by judicious

THE FASCIST SALUTE

Stiff Arm Society: Durham Blackshirts and German Rotarians exchange salutes, September 1933. Photo: Newcastle Chronicle & Journal

personal canvass." Those businessmen who responded to Fascism seemed more likely to adopt the Hopps or Idle semi-detached stance towards Mosley. An example was Col. K.C. Appleyard, a Birtley company director, who told a local meeting in November 1933 that Hitler, whilst wrong to expel the Jews from business, had done England and France a service by suppressing Communism, including presumably trade unions and co-operatives.

A similar attitude was shown in September 1934 when right-wing councillors, who were generally traders, tried to persuade South Shields

Council to drop a First World War ban on contracts with German firms. The move was foiled by an eloquent speech from a Labour councillor, Albert Gompertz. Confronted by Gompertz's anti-Nazi arguments, the mayor complained that "it was as well to forget such things" when it came to commerce. The former lord mayor of Newcastle, R.S. Dalgliesh, a shipowner of pronounced right-wing opinions, would have agreed. Dalgliesh demanded, in May 1936, the lifting of League of Nations trade sanctions imposed on Italy after Mussolini's invasion of Abyssinia. There was more where that came from.[13]

One further source of fascio-babble could be detected in a constant trickle of occasional sermons, letters to the local newspapers or comments by teachers. These outbursts, often thoughtless in their implications, could provoke brief controversy, as when a visiting Methodist preacher, David Pughe, praised Hitler in a talk at Sunderland in October 1933. But since the area's thriving array of daily, evening and weekly papers declined to follow the *Daily Mail* in recruiting for Fascism, the expression of pro-Nazi views remained subdued. The local press retained its mainstream Conservative loyalties. Apart from the publication of a couple of syndicated articles by Hitler in the *Newcastle Weekly Chronicle* in 1934, and a *Journal* editorial judgement that the Mosleyites should be allowed a hearing, press opinion on the Tyne and the Wear took a sharply critical view of Hitler, Mussolini and their creed.

The Armstrong Connection

Consequently, Fascist sympathisers in the business and civic spheres had to look elsewhere for encouragement. To an extent, two aging captains of industry were willing to nurture a degree of Fascist sentiment. Lord Armstrong, the Newcastle armaments magnate, had some kind words to say about Mosley. He told a Tory meeting at Scotswood Road's Ordnance Hotel in July 1934 that the Blackshirts "did good work" when they started, but felt that Mosley had taken a wrong turning by aping Mussolini. Armstrong maintained lucrative business relations with most Fascist regimes, and Vickers Armstrong was already selling war materials to the Nazis in October 1934, but one Tyneside connection was particularly curious.

In 1906, Armstrong helped to start a company at Wallsend with the aim of developing commercial applications for vitreous silica (used in the production of lighting globes and tubing). From 1916–1941, he chaired the main board of the company, known as Thermal Syndicate Limited. The firm deflected its German rivals by opening a Berlin subsidary in 1910 and, for the first year of the 1914–1918 war, the manager of the Berlin operation reported regularly to Wallsend via the company's New York sales office. Wartime dividends due to Thermal Syndicate from its Berlin offspring were protected by the German government and paid to the parent company in 1923. These rather neat arrangements, conducted whilst hundreds of thousands of Allied and German soldiers were ordered to slaughter each other in the bloodstained mud of Flanders, proved to be a fitting prelude to Thermal Syndicate's fortunes during the Nazi era.

Hitler's rise to power made little difference to Lord Armstrong and Thermal Syndicate. The Berliner Quarz-Schmelse G.m.b.h., as the German company was titled from 1935, was actually managed by a British national, Arthur Jepson, throughout the entire Second World War. Jepson had been born in Germany but derived British citizenship from his father. Subject to certain restrictions – he could not leave Berlin and had to report to a police station once a week – Jepson kept the factory working and was able to increase the order book. When the Nazis occupied France in 1940, the Berlin firm began to manage the affairs of Thermal Syndicate's French partner.

"Business as usual" was confirmed when the Nazi authorities in Berlin appointed trustees to look after Thermal Syndicate's interests. The trustees took their duties seriously, attending meetings of Berliner Quarz-Schmelse's shareholders and recording dividends and royalties for payment to Wallsend after the war. Unfortunately for Thermal Syndicate, the American Air Force bombed the trustees' records and the victorious Red Army confiscated the contents of the Berlin factory on their way back from closing down Hitler's bunker. But, undaunted, Jepson and Thermal Syndicate re-started production and subsequently enjoyed a good business relationship with Communist East Germany. Such are the epics of the twentieth century![14]

The Jarrow Killers

Meanwhile, back in the 1930s, Armstrong's equally elderly counterpart, Lord Runciman – "the veteran Tyneside shipowner" – had visited Italy and formed a favourable impression of Mussolini. Early in 1933, Runciman, the South Shields double-millionaire director of five shipping companies, made "a strong plea" for settling industrial disputes in "the Mussolini way".[15] For trade unionists, this would have sounded like an invitation to go directly to gaol. But Runciman's opinions carried a special weight due to his direct line to the Cabinet.

Lord Runciman's son, Walter, was President of the Board of Trade, rarely hesitating to use his position for the advantage of the family. Walter Runciman was party to the virtual destruction of Jarrow's economy in the early 1930s when he allowed the existence of an international steel cartel. This arrangement between steel producers to "manage" the market for their products had the effect of benefiting Nazi firms in Germany at the expense of Jarrow. Runciman and the cartel, adhering to the terms of the iron and steel companies' international agreement, prevented steel production from starting at Jarrow, where the economy had already been broken by shipyard closures. As a consequence, "the town that was murdered" in the graphic phrase coined by Jarrow's MP, Ellen Wilkinson, found that two-thirds of its industrial workers were thrown on the dole.

The Jarrow March 1936. Photo: Bede Gallery

Guy Waller, a contemporary journalist covering the famous Jarrow March of October 1936, which helped to draw attention to mass unemployment, accused Runciman of favouring Fascist regimes: "The British Fascists were far more deeply entrenched in the ranks of our industrialists and politicians than was ever publicly acknowledged." Waller argued that the government worked overtime to defuse the impact of the Jarrow March because it "quite unwittingly, posed the threat of exposing what can only be called The Fascist Connection." Whatever Runciman's aims, it was noteworthy that another member of the close-knit family, Walter Runciman's son (also named Walter), was a member of the Anglo-German Fellowship that cultivated extensive contacts with leading Nazis.[16]

The Londonderry Herr

An amalgam of business and politics on the Conservative Right did nourish a spectacular Nazi-connection in the person of Lord Londonderry. Charles Vane-Tempest-Stewart, 7th Marquess of Londonderry, heir to much of the Durham coalfield, and whose family had been reviled by generations of miners, was an ambitious man. He hoped to become Prime Minister and took his political apprenticeship in Northern Ireland where the Londonderry family owned substantial estates. As leader of the Northern Ireland Senate from 1921–26, Londonderry was associated with the gruesome creation of the Ulster statelet. This was a time when pogroms were conducted against the Catholic and Nationalist population with the connivance of the Ulster government's own security forces.

Londonderry served as Secretary of State for Air in the MacDonald Government from 1931, distinguishing himself at international disarmament conferences by defending the aerial bombing of Arab villages. This passion for bomber planes was his undoing. When Stanley Baldwin became Tory Prime Minister in 1935, Londonderry was sacked having become a political embarrassment for condoning atrocities as well as an obstacle to equipping the air force with fighters. Thereafter, Londonderry was mayor of Durham (1936–37), chancellor of the city's university, and president of the Conservative Party (1937). Above all, he became the principal Tory right-wing spokesman for the Nazis.

Freed from ministerial constraints, Londonderry spent three weeks in Berlin in January and February 1936, meeting Hitler, Goering and the ubiquitous Nazi diplomat, Ribbentrop. Two more trips quickly followed, enabling the Londonderrys to cement a growing friendship with Goering (they shared a fascination for warplanes and exchanged gifts of sheets dyed in air force blue). Londonderry, in defensive retrospect, dated his Nazi links to the period after he had left the British Government. However, the enthusiasm for Hitler's Germany had already gripped other members of the family. Lady Maureen Stanley, Londonderry's daughter and wife of Oliver Stanley, the Minister of Labour, visited the Nazi leaders Goebbels and Goering in October 1934 whilst her father was still a Minister. Soon after her return, Lady Maureen gleefully informed a Tory "political school" at Gateshead: "Germany is producing a magnificent race of young people and is managing to have a good time on very little money."[17]

When Londonderry came back from Berlin he told a reporter from the *Journal*: "I was much impressed by [Hitler's] popularity ... [he is] bold, energetic, patriotic, [and had] inspired the German people ... during the Nazi regime a marked change had come over the country." Asserting that Hitler wanted peace with Britain and France, Londonderry set out to echo Nazi foreign policy. At the height of the Spanish Civil War, and despite evidence of Nazi military intervention in the conflict, Londonderry spoke to the Seaham Harbour Conservative Club of his belief that Hitler was firm for peace and required "understanding".[18]

Cocktails And Nazis

Lady Londonderry shared the outlook of her husband and daughter. Following the first excursion to Germany, she wrote to Goering asking permission to call him "Siegfried" because she found him so dashing. The letter also identified English barriers to a rapport between Britain and Germany. These were the press ("controlled to a large extent by the Jews"), and friends of the Soviet Union ("all the Trade Unionists quite openly"). She pleaded with Goering to be patient about her slow efforts to "sway" public opinion: "You are fortunately in a strong position where you can command." Finally, Lady Londonderry was besotted with the Nazis, describing their first three years in power as producing "nothing less than a miracle".

Lord Londonderry (left) and friends (Hitler and Ribbentrop) in Berlin, 1937

The Londonderrys had the advantage of access to a glittering London cocktail circuit embracing the aristocracy, politicians, business and military leaders. They used their contacts to locate sympathisers and to promote Ribbentrop, who was to become Hitler's London ambassador. Ribbentrop and "a noisy gang of SS men" were guests of the Londonderrys at Mount Stewart, Northern Ireland, over Whitsun 1936. He visited again for three days in the autumn when they all had fun slaughtering 211 pheasants, a hare, eight rabbits, three woodcock and 28 ducks.[19]

There was one slight problem with this stratagem. Ribbentrop was a social disaster. He lacked polite graces and was apt to make a fool of himself. An example of this difficulty occurred in November 1936 when

Ribbentrop, weekending with the Londonderrys in the North East, joined the house party for Divine Service at Durham Cathedral. Mistaking a hymn tune for the German national anthem, Ribbentrop suddenly sprang into a Heil Hitler! salute, almost stopping the show. To the Londonderrys' great discomfort, Ribbentrop became widely regarded as "the Londonderry Herr".

Relentlessly, the Londonderrys pressed on. They invited Goering, whom they described as "a distinguished German", to stay with them for the 1937 Coronation. He declined, having realised that he would be made the ample target for anti-fascist protests. In 1938, Londonderry published *Ourselves and Germany*, a detailed defence of appeasement and the Nazis. The Penguin edition contained a publisher's note suggesting that readers should be made aware of unusual opinions. Displaying no such reservations, Londonderry highlighted "his particular gratitude to Herr Hitler, Field-Marshal Goring (*sic*), and Herr von Ribbentrop for their repeated kindness and hospitality to me and members of my family, as well for affording me many interesting sources of information." As an anti-semite ("I have no great affection for the Jews", Londonderry once told Ribbentrop), he still saw Hitler as the saviour of Europe.[20]

Third Reich Ltd

Londonderry was also involved with pro-Nazi pressure groups. Like the younger Runciman, he joined the Anglo-German Fellowship in 1935. The Fellowship's members encompassed many Tory MPs, Peers and company directors and several major firms such as Unilevers, Thomas Cook & Son and Firth-Vickers Stainless Steels (a subsidiary of the Tyneside-based Vickers Armstrong). Prominent Nazis were invited to address the Fellowship in London, and English members were hosted in Germany by Hitler and Goering. In January 1938, Londonderry together with other Fellowship members, signed a message of congratulation on the anniversary of the Nazi "revolution", which was published in the *Berliner Tageblatt*. Not suprisingly, Londonderry was connected with the more explicitly pro-Nazi group, The Link, formed in 1937. The Link was openly anti-semitic and published a journal entitled the *Anglo-German Review* to advertise Nazi ideas within the English Establishment.[21]

The details of Londonderry's complicity with Nazism would fill a large book but, interestingly, under Neville Chamberlain's Government from 1937, he was again offered public appointments. Chamberlain rewarded Londonderry by making him Chief Commissioner of the Civil Air Guard, and inviting Lady Londonderry to advise on female recruitment to the Territorial Army. At the same time, Londonderry retained a following among several Tory and National Liberal MPs on Tyneside. Thomas Magnay, the National Liberal MP for Gateshead sent a message of support to the *Anglo-German Review* in 1938, and Sir Alexander Russell, the Tory MP for Tynemouth, was a member of the Anglo-German Fellowship. Sir Nicholas Gratten-Doyle, a Newcastle Tory MP, wrote to *The Times* in 1934 defending Blackshirt violence at Mosley's rallies, arguing "is not the Fascists' psychology understandable?"

Another Tory MP, Alfred Denville (Newcastle Central), who was also an admirer of Mussolini, claimed at a 1938 public meeting in Chelsea Town Hall that the Spanish Fascists were "leading a crusade for all that they in England held dear." Denville's advocacy of Fascism in Spain merged with the Londonderrys' outlook. Lord and Lady Londonderry together with their son Viscount Castlereagh, MP, were all members of the Spanish Children's Repatriation Committee, a body dedicated to sending Basque refugee children, whose homes had been devastated by Nazi bombers, back to Fascist-held Spain.

It would be misleading to portray the whole of the Conservative Party in the image of Londonderry and his coterie. There were dissidents like Harold Macmillan, Anthony Eden and the young Edward Heath who took a stand against the pro-Nazi element. But it was Londonderry and people like him who exercised a strong influence on Tory thinking by 1938. If there was a "structure" of Fascist sympathisers waiting for their chance, as Tom Hadaway believed, then Londonderry was one of its lynchpins.

The outbreak of war with Germany in 1939, of course, put paid to the Londonderry design, but not to his survival instinct. With war raging in 1943, he published a self-serving little book, *Wings of Destiny*, breathtakingly re-writing some personal history: "I was openly accused of being a pro-Nazi ... on what grounds I have never been able to make out."[22]

4: STORM CENTRE

"Within the past three months" reported the Newcastle daily newspaper *The Journal,* in a special report on the BUF published on 9 May 1934, "Newcastle has achieved the unfortunate distinction of becoming one of the storm centres of aggressive Fascism in Great Britain. 'Storm-centre' is correct: Since 1 April of this year there have been no less than 14 street fights in Newcastle and Gateshead."

The tempo of Fascist violence had markedly accelerated following Mosley's visit to Durham at the end of 1933. In February 1934, the plate-glass windows of the Workers' Bookshop in Newcastle's Westgate Road were smashed by "young men seen to drive up to the shop in a car from which the number plates had been removed, hurl a brick at the window, and drive away." At Armstrong College, the virulent Fascist presence was accompanied by assaults on six individual students and the tearing down of Socialist posters.[23] These incidents, and others like them, had a deliberate intention: the intimidation of Fascism's opponents.

Central to the BUF's terror campaign was the introduction of a new North East leadership replacing Leaper and Risden. Ex-army officers clinging to war time titles were well to the fore. Captain Vincent Collier,

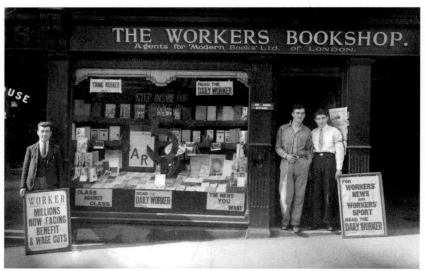

Anti-fascists: Workers' Bookshop, Westgate Road, Newcastle upon Tyne

who described himself as a "teacher of classics", has already been
mentioned and would have a consistent speaking and organising
presence. Above Collier stood Major E.W. Ormeston, formerly of the
Durham Light Infantry, who, assisted by Captain Vincent Keens, was "in
control of Fascism in Newcastle and on Tyneside."

Collier's anti-semitism was bad enough but an especially nasty piece of
work could be found in Captain J. Bruce-Norton, the BUF's Area
Political Officer. Bruce-Norton was a Fascist fanatic (so, too, was his
wife). After the 1914–18 war, he joined the Royal Irish Constabulary's
Auxiliary Division, successors to the notorious Black and Tans, charged
with suppressing the Irish independence movement in 1920–21.
Defeated in Ireland, Bruce-Norton then found work as a probably
distasteful colonial officer in Africa, and on returning to England he
instantly joined Mosley.[24]

Moran And Beckett

Recreating the officer-corps legacy of the British Fascisti may have
impressed Fascists in their Newcastle and Durham club rooms. But the
BUF's chief objective on the Tyne and the Wear was to break the Labour
Movement, part of a concerted effort to penetrate working class areas,
and this required more than ex-officers. Thinking that he understood the
needs of the situation, Mosley drafted two of his key lieutenants whom he
supposed might continue the strategy of Leaper, Risden and Miles.

Mosley decided to send Tommy Moran back to Tyneside in January
1934. Moran was an ex-miner (though he was sometimes described as
an engineer) and hailed from Newcastle's Scotswood Road. He had
joined the BUF in July 1933, resigning a Labour Party secretaryship,
possibly at Derby but he had held office in the Newcastle West
Divisional Labour Party. Moran was also a former cruiserweight boxing
champion in the Royal Navy, a useful background for someone who was
to spend most of the 1930s getting into brawls. Colin Cross, in his fine
book *The Fascists in Britain*, noted that Moran had "ambitions to be an
intellectual rather than a strong-arm man." In any event, Moran's
usefulness to Mosley lay in his Geordie and Labour background and his
"outstanding" organising skills. By 1 May 1934, the Newcastle police
were considering whether to arrest Moran for incitement to violence.

But John Beckett was Mosley's greatest "catch" for his North East design. Beckett had been an ILP parliamentary candidate for Newcastle North and subsequently served as an ILP Member of Parliament for Gateshead from 1924–29. He had a wealth of Labour experience behind him – as a Labour councillor in Hackney, a policy adviser to the ILP and private secretary and election agent for Clement Attlee, a future Labour leader and Prime Minister. Beckett left Gateshead in 1929 for "political and personal reasons" and was elected as an ILP MP for Peckham in the general election of that year. He remained loyal to the ILP at the 1931 election and lost his seat.

Nothing up my sleeve: John Beckett makes a point. Photo: Francis Beckett

Like Mosley, Beckett had tired of the parliamentary scene and was impressed by Mussolini's Italian Fascism. At the same time, as Colin Cross records, Beckett was losing interest in organised labour: "Fifteen years in the working-class movement have taught me that the workmen want security. They do not want to govern … Manliness, courage, thought and discipline are weapons with which security, peace and comfort can be obtained." Beckett's fermenting anti-semitism, too, may have played a part in his transition to Fascism. Ironically, his mother was Jewish (a fact concealed by Beckett), but had been excluded by her ultra-orthodox family for marrying a gentile. Maybe this sowed seeds of resentment in Beckett. In any event, he was also greatly frustrated by his failure as an MP to call the Jewish manufacturer, Sir Alfred Mond, to public account for exploiting German chemical secrets obtained after the First World War.

Three British army officers had prepared a report on German methods of extracting nitrogen from the air, and this had been presented to the government of which Mond was a member. The officers' report then disappeared from government files and, soon afterwards, a Mond-owned company employing the ex-officers began utilising the German processes, making vast profits for Mond. No matter how hard he tried, Beckett could not touch Mond. The failure infuriated Beckett, a former soldier, who saw this as an example of profiteering over the bodies of his dead former comrades in the trenches.

At the beginning of March 1934, Beckett was recruited to the BUF by Robert Forgan, another one-time Labour MP turned Fascist. Moving straight on to Mosley's extensive payroll, Beckett was despatched to Tyneside and, by the middle of May, he and Moran claimed to have held 60 local meetings.[25]

'The Corner Ends'

The organisation that Moran, Beckett and the "officer-corps" were building looked sizeable. The *Journal* report on the BUF judged that Fascist numbers in Newcastle were "greatly overestimated" but were probably around 500 if nominal members "and women Blackshirts" were included. A "large proportion" of the Newcastle and Gateshead membership were unemployed – possibly attracted by Mosley's ability to pay Blackshirts for part-time work – and the bulk of the North East members "consisted of energetic youths who probably have little or no knowledge of the politics of the Party", explaining why efficient platform speakers "are few and far between."

Details of the BUF membership are still difficult to obtain but general press reports of disturbances at Fascist meetings, and naming particular Blackshirts, tend to confirm the *Journal's* impression. Cyril Nicholson, a Fascist from Queensway, in Newcastle's Fenham suburb, who was "felled" at a local BUF meeting in April 1934, was 18 years of age. John Dalgleish, the BUF organiser at 28 West Sunniside, Sunderland in 1933–34, was described in the *Sunderland Echo* as a "youth". A particularly active Blackshirt, John Theodorson, was an officer of the Newcastle BUF. In May 1934, he claimed that he was assaulted at a Sunderland Fascist meeting, then "felled" by a broken bottle at Newcastle and, in July, he was punched by an angry crowd at North Shields. Theodorson was a student at Armstrong College.

Similarly, a Labour Party survey of the BUF conducted in mid-1934 produced a picture of the Newcastle Fascists as "largely a youth movement" of "young chaps attracted by the sporting side (boxing, etc)." Other observers were less neutral. Two County Durham miners, recalling the Fascists of the 1934–35 period, offered down-to-earth descriptions. Fenwick Whitfield, watching the Fascists march out of their Lovaine Place lair, said they were "what we call 'the corner ends'. The chap who would be standing around on the street corner ... Fellas with no opinion at all, bruisers ... boxers and ex-boxers ... strong in the back and no brains." For George Bestford, the Fascists' recruits had a simple outlook: "Give them a uniform and a bloody drum and they'll follow for miles. That was the attraction of the Fascist Party ... the uniform and knocking the hell out of a drum." Terence Monaghan, an unemployed Tyneside fitter in the 1930s, believed the local Blackshirts "around Mosley at his meetings were all known for what they were – they were a lot of villains."

A prime task of the Blackshirted youth was to "protect" Fascist speakers at outdoor meetings. Tom Callaghan, in his autobiography *A Lang Way to the Pa'nshop*, remembered as a child seeing BUF meetings at Benwell and Newcastle's Bigg Market: "the uniformed Blackshirts ranged themselves around the platform as a token of security; their arms folded, and grim faced, each of them had that particular expression upon their countenance, that certain look" which, combined with the wide leather belts and large buckles worn as potential weapons over their black outfits, presented a threatening aura. Tom Callaghan also recalled that the Mosleyites' para-military displays had an unforseen impact on audiences: "It was their militant appearance, and their fierce address, that appeared to convince me, that as a political party, they somehow antagonized the majority of their audience... who united in their hostility towards the Fascists, putting aside their own political differences for the moment. And, of course, at such times the scenes could be quite ugly!"

Street Fights

Displays of Blackshirt muscle were not necessarily effective. Sunderland, like Newcastle's Bigg Market, found the Fascists provocative and Blackshirt meetings were stopped in their tracks in February 1934 and again in May. But Newcastle was the "storm centre" where the Fascists reaped an angry backlash. Street meetings in the town centre were "attended with a good deal of disorder" in early March, and in mid-April Moran, advised by the police to close an open-air meeting, retreated with 34 Blackshirts to his Clayton Street offices, "the column broken several times and the size of the crowd stopped all the traffic." Moran, typically, blamed the Communists "assisted by a number of Jews", but the Fascist newspaper *Fascist Week* admitted that "opposition is making itself felt."

Things were going from bad to worse when "the rowdiest gathering in the history of the Fascist movement in Newcastle" resulted in Moran again scuttling back to Clayton Street "followed along the entire route by a procession of jeering antagonists." The *Journal* reported that "Blackshirt-baiting" had assumed the status of "a new Sunday night pastime" and *Fascist Week*, driven to distraction, complained that a Blackshirt meeting had been seen off amidst "a shower of whelk and winkle shells." By May, some 40 Fascists had been injured and 11 had required hospital treatment.[26]

Anti-Fascists

The strength of the anti-fascist opposition hinted that the shock of the Blackshirts' violent emergence in 1933 was being overcome. There is evidence of a patchwork of anti-fascist groupings becoming active over the winter of 1934. The National Unemployed Workers' Movement was one example. Organising many of the area's unemployed miners, engineering and shipyard workers, fighting cuts in the "dole", providing social centres and staging protest "Hunger Marches", the NUWM secured a large following. Fascist tactics, targeting the NUWM as "Red subversion", overlooked the tangible benefits gained by the organisation for the unemployed. Consequently, the Movement and those CP and ILP members among its activists, found unemployed workers and their families more than willing to harass the BUF. This was noticeably true at Sunderland, North Shields and Felling where the NUWM had a powerful presence.

Where the NUWM was weaker, as in Newcastle, South Shields and Gateshead, other labour organisations took a pronounced part in opposing the Blackshirts. The miners' lodges formed a bedrock of anti-fascism in the South Shields, Bolden, Jarrow and Northumberland

HITLER TO BRITISH FASCISM : "The first thing is to foster division among the workers—after that it is easy."

New Leader, 31 March 1933

areas. A North East Anti-Fascist Committee, instigated by the Durham Miners' Association at Gateshead in May 1933, appears to have had a temporary co-ordinating role, and the Northumberland Miners' Association reacted quickly to counter racist propaganda circulated by the English Mistery group in villages such as Broomhill in May 1934.

Similarly, trades councils, connecting most union branches in each borough across the Tyne and the Wear, adopted an anti-fascist stance. Newcastle Trades Union Council, accepting that Fascism may seem small in Britain felt "we must not be silent" in the teeth of "dictatorships which have crushed noble men and women." The Council tried to initiate a move against Fascism early in 1934 but met with little response from the Newcastle City Labour Party. The Party "turned down" the Trades Council's proposed "joint campaign", being "inclined to ignore the Fascists altogether" and "preach Socialism" instead.

In marked contrast, South Shields Trades Council, which was linked with the town's Labour Party, mounted frequent anti-fascist meetings in Shields Market Place. At neighbouring Jarrow, the joint Jarrow Labour Party and Trades Council also moved against the Fascists. A.A. Rennie, the Council's secretary, replied to the Labour Party survey that the BUF had started a Felling branch of "between 20 & 30 strong", but this soon collapsed, and Fascist meetings had been held "in Hebburn (crowd attacked the speaker & badly mauled him since when no further attempt has been made) and in Jarrow (crowd kept up a volley of noise & compelled the speaker to desist)."[27]

As winter turned to spring in 1934, the Blackshirts found themselves confronted by an array of opposition. Not necessarily co-ordinated, the anti-fascists were meeting the challenge both politically and physically. Trade unions, political parties, and unemployed groups were forging a coalition pledged to stop Mosley's men in their tracks. And central to this coalition was something that the Mosleyites had never really envisaged. Anti-fascism, as it happened, had an additional and powerful element.

42

5: THE FEMALE TOUCH

It is easy though misleading to regard the conflict between British Fascism and anti-fascism in the 1930s as no more than a series of street fights and rowdy meetings. Viewed in this way, anti-fascism can be seen as a very male preserve, especially as the men were generally the most visible on the "physical force" side of anti-fascism. In fact, women were often evident in the anti-fascist crowd scenes as well, and their comprehensive presence in the struggle has been invariably overlooked. Women were greatly concerned about Fascism. The threat posed to working class communities and organisations agitated women on the Tyne and the Wear, but their response to Fascism also took into account the broader tenets of Fascist ideology. In short, those women who wanted more out of life than domestic servility and endless child-rearing quickly realised the danger of allowing Fascist influence to grow unchecked. The emergence of a militant and enduring Fascist party, against the dreary background of British conservatism in the 'thirties, would stifle women's efforts to secure equality with men. Consequently, women became a significant ingredient in anti-fascism.

Red Ellen

The woman who symbolised female anti-fascism perhaps more than most on Tyneside and beyond, was Ellen Wilkinson, the Labour parliamentary candidate for unemployment-stricken Jarrow, and the town's MP from 1935. Small, red haired and equipped with a dynamic personality, Ellen Wilkinson started her political life in the ILP in 1912, worked for the women's suffrage movement and briefly joined the Communist Party in the early 1920s. As an organiser for the shop workers' trade union, she attacked injustices affecting women workers, and carried the case for improving women's rights at work into the Labour Party. From 1924 until 1931, she was a Labour MP for Middlesbrough.

Ellen Wilkinson is usually associated with memories of the famous Jarrow March of 1936 which, among the Hunger Marches of the period, carved the scandal of unemployment into the political agenda. But Wilkinson also gave anti-fascism an extraordinarily high profile in her activities at home and abroad, occasionally risking severe censure

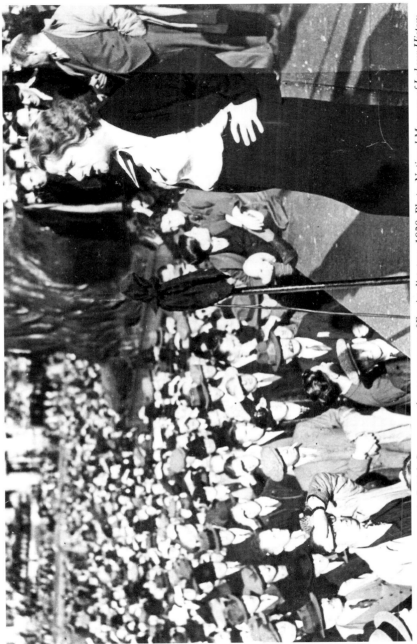

Ellen Wilkinson denounces the British Government's appeasement of Fascist dictators, 1938. Photo: National Museum of Labour History

by her own party's leaders who tended to see the issue as a Communist-inspired distraction. Refusing to be deflected from anti-fascism, she worked with the German Social-Democrats in the violent electoral contest with Hitler in 1932–33, and organised support for those whom the Nazis persecuted.

"Red Ellen", as she was nicknamed, arranged an important anti-fascist conference at Jarrow in April 1934, attracting 600 delegates and addressed by the German Socialist refugee, Edward Conze. Lecturing frequently for the left-wing adult education body, the National Council of Labour Colleges, Conze provided valuable first-hand knowledge of Fascist methods for trade union and Labour Party branches all over the country.

Wilkinson and Conze co-operated to alert the Labour Movement to the Nazi menace. In 1934, they were joint authors of a book, *Why Fascism?* The significance of *Why Fascism?* rested in its development of the basic analysis of Fascism found on the British Left. Although agreeing that Fascism was a product of a crisis-riven capitalism, and as a party of order held obvious attractions for governments desperate to prevent social revolution, Wilkinson and Conze paid particular attention to the ideological challenge posed by Mosley. Socialist and Communist critics of Fascism often accepted that numbers of middle and working class people could be attracted to Mosley out of a desire for a restoration of stability, but this argument failed to explain why the BUF recruited from the Left with apparent ease. To label former Socialist or Communist recruits to Fascism as "traitors" or "turncoats" might explain the behaviour of individuals, but was hardly an adequate interpretation of a somewhat larger phenomenon.

Why Fascism? located Mosley's appeal in his promotion of a Corporate State which, superficially at least, embraced economic planning, public expenditure to reduce unemployment, and a strong role for the state in imposing the "common good" over business interests. These ideas, argued Wilkinson and Conze, could encourage Socialists disenchanted with MacDonald, alienated by Russian Communism and disheartened by the ILP's lurch into the "wilderness", to cross over into a Fascism headed by former "comrades". Certainly, this seems to have been a strong factor in John Beckett's transition to Fascism, since he saw continuity between his ILP Socialism and the "earnest Socialist conviction" he claimed to find in the BUF. The anti-fascist response, Wilkinson and Conze believed, should be one of exposing what the Corporate State meant in practice in Italy and Germany, and persuading the British Labour Movement that it must adopt a stronger Socialist commitment.

Socialist League

Another key component of the broad anti-fascist coalition coming together on Tyneside in 1934 was the Socialist League. A network of League branches emanating from Gateshead contained the more radical members of the Labour Party and enjoyed widespread support in the Tyneside constituency parties. The League acted, to some extent, as an unofficial bridge with the ILP (which had its own premises at the Westfield Hall, Gateshead) and, despite differences, with the Communist Party as well.

An advantage for the League was access to a well-produced and readable monthly newspaper, the *Gateshead Herald*. The paper was the voice of the Gateshead Labour Party but mainly the responsibility of Ruth Dodds, a local Labour councillor and stalwart of many progressive causes. Ruth Dodds ensured that anti-fascism was treated seriously by the *Herald* and this meant that the Socialist League had a shop window for its contribution.

Interestingly, the Socialist League's anti-fascism also highlighted the place of women in opposing Fascism. The League operated a women's group in 1933–34 and, from the end of 1933, League members presented a series of meetings designed to unite anti-fascists on the Left. Ellen Wilkinson addressed a large public meeting at the Westfield Hall on "Workers and Women Under Fascism" in December 1933, and Constance Barrett, a former Suffragette and Labour parliamentary candidate, delivered a Socialist League lecture on the evils of Fascism at the People's Theatre, then at Newcastle's Rye Hill, in March 1934. Among other meetings held by the League was one in June 1934 attracting 150 people to hear a female German Socialist refugee at Chester-le-Street. "Chester-le-Street had never seen a more enthusiastic meeting" said the *Herald*.

Ellen Wilkinson In Gateshead

THE NEED FOR UNITY

Comrade Mary Gunn presided at a packed meeting at Westfield Hall last month, when Ellen Wilkinson spoke at a meeting organised by the Socialist League on the Fascist menace. She traced the Hitler terror, with all its horrors, to the weakness of divided Socialist forces in Germany. Her pictures of countries under Fascist tyranny led on to an eloquent appeal to the Socialist Movement in this country to take warning; we are not the inheritors of the old party tradition of ins and outs with no fundamental differences, we must be prepared to take control of every instrument of power in the country, when the people gave us the right, and use them all for the establishment of the commonwealth of all.

A resolution was passed demanding the acquittal of Torgler and the Bulgarians in the Reichstag trial, and that they should be allowed to leave Germany unmolested. The deputation, consisting of an I.L.P.er, a Communist and a Labour councillor, took this resolution next day to the German Consul at Newcastle. The Communists have been acquitted; but they are still in prison in Germany, and no one can feel assured of their safety.

Gateshead Herald, January 1934

Leah Manning

Nor was female participation in anti-fascism confined to Tyneside. On Wearside, women anti-fascists were certainly part of the opposition at Blackshirt meetings. But just as Ellen Wilkinson played a notable public role on Tyneside, so another Labour parliamentary candidate, Leah Manning, was to the fore in challenging Fascism in Sunderland. Adopted as a Labour candidate for one of Sunderland's two parliamentary seats in 1933, Leah Manning had been a Labour MP, briefly, for East Islington until the 1931 election disaster. Those who knew Manning recalled her as "a tall, solidly-built, rather majestic person, with a ready smile and lively personality" and "a great crusader on a variety of platforms … a rebel, a feminist and a forceful and outspoken voice of the Left." She served as president of the National Union of Teachers from 1929, following several years intense campaigning for wider educational opportunities for working class children through the National Association of Labour Teachers. During the 1930s, Manning was deeply involved with anti-fascism and, in 1934, became a joint secretary of the left-wing Co-ordinating Committee Against War and Fascism. She worked ceaselessly to assist refugees from Nazi Germany and, later, dedicated herself to aiding Spanish resistance to Fascist threats.

This determination led Leah Manning to link closely with Ellen Wilkinson as well as to make common cause with all anti-fascists. It was a decision that exposed her to being branded as a Communist by some of the Labour Party's leaders, more concerned with keeping the CP at arms-length, and who then attempted to undermine her position within the NUT. The attacks were taken up in Sunderland by the town's Labour Party Executive Committee which, in May 1935, saw her "called over the coals" for sharing platforms with CP and ILP speakers. Her difficulties were compounded when the other Labour candidate for Sunderland, the left-wing lawyer D.N. Pritt, resigned. His place was taken by the Labour right-winger, George Catlin, father of Shirley Williams.

Catlin and Manning shared a curious political partnership. Manning stood firmly for international labour solidarity in the fight against economic slump and Fascism. Catlin, in contrast, was wedded to a narrow, conservative "patriotism" in the belief that this could beat the Tories. He even draped his public meetings in Union Jack flags! Meanwhile, a nasty Tory smear was launched against Manning in Sunderland, aimed at persuading the town's large Catholic population that Manning was in favour of talking openly about sex and love. The result of the smear and Labour disunity was that both Manning and Catlin were defeated at the 1935 general election by two businessmen, one Liberal and one Tory, standing on a "National Government" ticket.

Leah Manning's supporters did persuade the Sunderland Labour Party to offer her a renewed candidacy after 1935. However, she judged that commuting to Sunderland at weekends from her home and job in London, and fighting to defend her growing enthusiasm for anti-fascism against constant sniping from Labour bigwigs, was untenable. She therefore turned away from parliamentary ambitions for the rest of the 1930s and concentrated substantial energies on the NUT and aid for Spain.

Women Against Fascism

A distinctive feature of anti-fascism on Tyneside and Wearside was the prominence achieved by women at a time when politics was very much a male preserve. Apart from Ellen Wilkinson, Ruth Dodds and the Socialist League and Leah Manning, women made their views felt in other settings. Two ILP members, Allie Livingstone and Poin Sedgewick, both aged about 17 years, were active anti-fascists in Gateshead by January 1934. And the first appearance of the Blackshirts at North Shields, when a Fascist was invited to address a debating society, brought a sharp response from local women. Jenny Goldsack and a Mrs. E. Badsey, spurning the possibility of violent Fascist retribution, took the quite brave steps of writing at length to the *Shields News* castigating Fascism's treatment of women as mere domestic objects and criticising the BUF's anti-semitism and hostility towards democracy and the trade unions.

There were other women, too, who grasped the relevance of anti-fascism, and in somewhat surprising ways. Hilda Ashby, who grew up in a mining family at Chopwell (County Durham's "Little Moscow"), and worked as a cinema cleaner and usherette in the village during the mid-1930s, went youth hostelling in Hitler's Germany in 1935. The experience stimulated her keen opposition to Fascism. Similarly, Connie Lewcock, a former Newcastle Suffragette, went camping in northern Spain in 1932 and was impressed by popular enthusiasm for the new democracy that the Fascists were already plotting to destroy.

And then there was Emmie Lawther, a trade unionist from the Potteries who moved to Chopwell in 1923 (her husband, whom she had met whilst they were students at the Labour Movement's Ruskin College in 1920–22, came from a large family of radical trade unionists at Chopwell). Emmie Lawther took an active part in the Labour Party's women's sections from 1924, and organised community support for the trade unions during the 1926 General Strike in the Blaydon area. Later in the 1920s, she set up a campaign for women to have access to birth control. This brought criticism from male Labour MPs, especially when Lawther breast-fed her four-month old daughter at a Labour Party national conference after speaking to a resolution advocating birth control. As the 1930s unfolded, she helped to organise unemployed Hunger Marches to London.

Described by other Labour women as "outspoken and intellectual", Emmie Lawther's awareness of the Fascist danger emerged very early and took her to the first International Anti-Fascist Congress held at Berlin in 1929. A year spent teaching English in Vienna after leaving Ruskin College had also given her a grasp of German which came in useful during the rise of Nazism. Shortly after Hitler came to power, Emmie Lawther fostered an eight-years old refugee from the Nazis who, thirteen years later as a British soldier, was at last reunited with his own mother in the ruins of Berlin.[28]

This explosive mixture of women anti-fascists with labour organisations, all convinced that they were engaged in a life-or-death struggle, generated a tension on the Tyne and the Wear in the early part of 1934. Something was bound to happen.

WRITERS FOR LIBERTY

The 1930s saw many writers – poets, novelists, playwrights – taking a stand against Fascism. Since the Nazis' notorious public book burnings clearly indicated Fascism's celebration of ignorance and bigotry, the very survival of literature as a source of independent criticism was at stake. At the time, there was not a lot of scope for earning a living as a writer on Tyneside, so the area's authors generally had to leave for London and further afield. Two of these "exiles" faced up to Fascism with distinction and in very different ways.

Jack Common

Jack Common, the son of a railwayman, was born at Heaton, Newcastle upon Tyne, in 1903. He learned about life as a child on the streets, briefly as a "confidential clerk to a drunken solicitor", and then during three years on the dole. In 1928 he went to London, worked as a mechanic and then joined a literary magazine, *The Adelphi*, "as circulation man." Within a year, Common was assistant editor and, in 1936, he became acting editor. Bringing a set of sharp insights into social reality to the London literary and left-wing scene, Common marked out a place for himself as a writer and commentator drawing upon his own background. His account of working lives in **Seven Shifts**, published at the end of the 'thirties, his subsequent film work and his autobiography of childhood, **Kiddar's Luck**, written in the 1950s are monuments of working class writing.

Jack Common wanted a better society. He saw the possibility of a Socialism developed out of the hopes and aspirations of working men and women rather than planned and imposed by political bureaucrats. For this reason, he was attracted by the Independent Labour Party's belief that cultivating personal values of equality and sensitivity within "communities in which classlessness is a virtue and is understood in all its forms" was as necessary as any party programme.

But nothing could be built if Fascism won. In his book **Freedom of the Streets**, published in 1938 and drawing upon articles in *The Adelphi*, Jack Common noted the ambivalence of the English Establishment towards Fascism: "At one moment they think fascism is just the thing for them: it will recapture their power for them and beat off the hands of the workers ... At the next they think no, democracy is the only safeguard: it 'has' served us well." Common saw Fascism as holding attractions for small business people, losing economic status because of competition from large corporations and mass production. Much of his literary effort, therefore, was geared towards outlining a new common culture capable of replacing the divisive social and economic system that generated Fascist ideas.

[See: Huw Beynon and Colin Hutchinson (eds), **Jack Common's Revolt Against An 'Age of Plenty'**, Strongwords, Newcastle upon Tyne, 1980]

Elinor Brent-Dyer

Elinor Brent-Dyer was quite different from Jack Common. Born at South Shields in 1894, she came from a middle-class family made relatively poor by her father's desertion. Educated at Leeds Training College, she became a teacher at the Boys' High School in South Shields, and later opened the Margaret Roper Girls' School, Hereford. In 1925 she published the first of her Chalet School stories, the beginning of a literary epic that eventually included 58 books about a fictional girls' boarding school in the Austrian Tyrol.

The world of the Chalet School combines convincing descriptions of the Austrian landscape with a cheery, international schoolgirl community. Easy to read, there is a continuity between the books (characters who appear as schoolgirls in the early stories ultimately send their own children to the Chalet School), cementing the reader's awareness of a privileged, *bourgeois* society that would have been anathema to Jack Common from the railway streets of Heaton.

But there was one thing that Brent-Dyer shared with Common: a deep antipathy towards Fascism. According to one Brent-Dyer biography, the Chalet School series "sought to evangelize against English parochialism and xenophobia" during a period when hostility towards foreigners was rampant.

Brent-Dyer was always at great pains to point out that there was a difference between ordinary German people and the Nazis. This perspective laid the foundations for a forceful anti-Nazi stand, beginning with **Exploits of the Chalet Girls** (1933) which explicitly warned against "Hitler and his works." Perhaps "the best single title was **The Chalet School in Exile** (1940), a horrific if judicious account of the school's flight from Nazi rule with a grimly realistic depiction of homicidal persecution of Jews." The girls go to the aid of a Jewish man who is being chased and stoned by a Nazi rabble, and then they have to flee from the Nazi police and army.

While other children's writers ignored Nazism, Elinor Brent-Dyer mobilised her "girls" to sock the Third Reich firmly on the chin. Her anti-Nazi emphasis was almost unique in children's fiction writing in the 1930s.

Elinor Brent-Dyer died in 1969 but her books, never out of print, sell more than 150,000 copies a year.

[See: Helen McClelland, **Behind the Chalet School**, Anchor, London, 1986]

6: TURNING POINT:
THE ANTI-FASCIST LEAGUE

On a Thursday evening, 10 May 1934, there took place in a meeting hall above 2 Blandford Street, Newcastle upon Tyne, a gathering of some import for the fortunes of Mosley's men on Tyneside. In an intriguing incident, proposals carrying considerable implications were decided by people whose exact identities, beliefs, anger and hopes are now lost to human memory. But one definite item stood out: the anti-fascists who met at Blandford Street were men and women who, in Oliver Cromwell's phrase about an earlier generation of libertarians, "knew what they fought for and loved what they knew."

SOCIALIST DEFENCE CORPS

New League in Newcastle

A league has been formed in Newcastle this week, the main purpose of which is to provide uniformed protection for speakers at Socialist meetings. The league is also sworn to encourage and give hospitality to refugees from Fascism in other countries, and, as far as possible, to prevent Jewish pogroms.

The league is stated to be open to all grades of Socialists who believe in democratic methods, and is called the Anti-Fascist League. Although the first meeting was only held at 2, Blandford Street last Thursday it already claims to have 200 members in the district.

The league is to form a defence corps, and a meeting to decide the uniform is to be held next week. No names are at present being divulged, but a *Newcastle Journal* representative was informed by one of the committee last night that the league is to join with similar organizations in other centres.

Newcastle Journal, 12 May 1934

Fortunately, a keen-eyed reporter on the *Journal* had the nous to ask one of the Blandford Street group a few questions. It had been resolved to provide "uniformed protection at Socialist meetings", as well as to oppose anti-semitism, by forming an Anti-Fascist League. About 200 people had joined. Tom Brown, a County Durham Syndicalist remembered by his London Anarchist comrades of the 1930s for his "commonsense" witty and logical style of public speaking, wrote half a century later that the League's members were "almost exclusively working class with fifty per cent of that out of work." Support came also from "two prominent members of the Labour Party...both full-time officials of the Transport and General Workers' Union." Reflecting the habits of the times, the AFL's members wore grey shirts and "marches showed that the older men remembered their military life in World War One." Public meetings were held and, as Tom Brown recalled, "our members, singly, or in pairs, interviewed Fascist recruits and in most cases persuaded them to pack it in."[29]

The AFL was predictably slated in the Tory press as "disgraceful and intolerable" for displaying "every device" of the Socialists in opposing the Blackshirts, but the organisation grew stronger. Periodically, "a party of Greyshirts" could be "seen in the city streets" on watch for Fascist meetings. The AFL secretary, A. Chater, wrote in the *Journal*: "Our organisation has no connection with any political party. Inside our ranks will be found all shades of political opinion, each and every one determined to extinguish" the Fascist threat to life, liberty and freedom.[30]

Chater wrote from the Smiths' Hall, Monk Street, Newcastle, where the AFL had rented an office and held its own physical training sessions. Tom Brown noted that local residents "kept an eye on the premises at night. Many of these good people were street sellers and offered their barrows and carts to form quick barricades if the Fascists attacked. Some of them, such as newspaper sellers who worked in and around the Central Station, were able to keep us informed of Fascist visitors to the area." This was not an inconsequential point since, as Len Edmondson recalled, the Fascists sometimes imported thugs *via* the station for meetings at the nearby Cowen's Monument.

May Day And After

The immediate impetus for the convening of the Blandford Street meeting stemmed from the recent experience of the ILP. On 1 May 1934, the ILP had staged a May Day meeting outside the Gateshead Labour Exchange at Windmill Hills. Whilst the meeting was in progress, a line of Blackshirts chanting "M-O-S-L-E-Y" appeared, heading towards the ILP rostrum and with crystal clear intentions. Not for the first time, the Fascists misjudged the mood of unemployed workers. The dole queue waiting outside the Exchange turned and about 1000 men rushed the Mosleyites, one of whom was "knocked unconscious" and another "lost two teeth." The Blackshirts fled.[31]

By threatening a May Day meeting, celebrating the international unity of workers facing common problems of economic slump and Fascism, the BUF unwittingly produced an entirely new situation. Instead of responding to Fascist violence, the strategy of anti-fascism on Tyneside now changed to one of completely breaking the BUF. The Anti-Fascist

League was to be the instrument of the new departure, leading directly to some of the largest political confrontations of the 1930s: the Tyneside anti-fascist demonstrations of 13 and 14 May 1934.

From Cowen's Monument ...

The Fascist organisers John Beckett and Tommy Moran planned to raise the temperature with a series of major rallies in Newcastle and Gateshead, culminating in a gigantic event with Mosley on the Town Moor during Race Week. Anti-fascists resolved to stop them. On Sunday 13 May, some 30 Fascists left their Clayton Street office *en route* for a Beckett meeting at Cowen's Monument. There were scuffles, then uproar due to an attack on a Communist worker in Blackett Street, rolling into another fight along Westgate Road. The *Journal* (14 May) reported that "several of the Blackshirts pursued their opponents into doorways, knocked them down, and were in turn struck down." At Cowen's Monument, a "crowd of several thousands" was gathering and this "enormous crowd refused to give Mr. Beckett a hearing" and called him "a traitor." Beckett recalled in his autobiography that a thousand anti-fascists rushed his platform and "pandemonium broke loose."

The police believed that the AFL, whose members were present but not wearing their grey shirts, was behind the anti-fascist demonstration, and they told Beckett and Moran to abandon the meeting. The BUF attempted to retire to Clayton Street "carrying two men, and two more were unconscious before we had gone far" wrote Beckett. Mounted police were then instructed to escort the Blackshirts back to BUF headquarters. The anti-fascists did not go away, but laid siege to the Fascists' offices, placing it "under a steady rain of missiles." According to Beckett, "every window" was broken and "the large branch room, with its floor covered in blood and groaning men, was a gruesome sight."

An hour or so later, twenty Blackshirts rushed out of their building intent on attacking the crowd and "rescuing" two or three of their comrades. They succeeded only in getting the worst of the encounter and in seeing two of their number arrested. Eventually, the furore died away and the anti-fascists dispersed, many to the Palace Theatre in Newcastle's Haymarket to hear James Maxton, a fiery Glasgow ILP MP, call for a united front against Fascism.

…To Gateshead And Back

Back at Clayton Street, where the atmosphere inside the BUF offices resembled the last moments of the Alamo, judging from the report of a *North Mail* journalist trapped inside the premises, Beckett and Moran prepared for their next move. The following evening, Beckett was due to address a large rally at Gateshead Town Hall, playing upon the former MP's local reputation. Although Gateshead's right-wing town council had allowed the Fascists to hire the Town Hall, Beckett was not certain of a friendly welcome. And when he arrived with thirty two Blackshirts, who were apparently armed with rubber bludgeons and pieces of steel wrapped in cloth, he found a hostile "crowd of thousands" surrounding the building.

A strong police cordon got Beckett into the Hall where he found an audience of a hundred "active Fascists (50 in uniform)" and 150 anti-fascist hecklers. There followed a limp speech by a dejected Beckett, enlivened only by his advocacy of concentration camps, and then the Blackshirts cut their losses. Outside the Hall, Beckett encountered "the largest crowd that has ever assembled for a rally of this kind on Tyneside, and solidly lining West Street, the High Street" and the length of the Tyne Bridge.

The police had to clear a path for Beckett's escape: "Crowds of more than 10,000 people were driven back and 60 fascists were escorted to their headquarters by mounted police and motor cycle patrols", according to the *News Chronicle*. As the Blackshirts got half-way across the Tyne Bridge "a section of the crowd attempted to rush the party" seemingly intending to throw the Fascists into the river. Prevented from reaching the Blackshirts by the police, "several thousands followed [Beckett] to Clayton Street", blockading the BUF offices for a second night. "I have participated in no stormier scene" said Beckett, looking back at his two nights on Tyneside.[32]

The demonstrations of 13 and 14 May brought BUF activity to a virtual halt. Beckett held a small meeting at Whitley Bay and odd, unannounced, open-air meetings were tried at Wallsend's Borough Field. But in late-May the BUF confirmed that no meetings at all were being arranged, commenting sourly that "Newcastle is apparently the only place where an Englishman is not allowed the much vaunted privilege of free speech." Among Fascists, the AFL's success caused consternation, and national officers of the BUF were "sent to investigate conditions in Newcastle." It later emerged that Mosley secretly "paid a hurried visit" to the city, alarmed at the effects of the anti-fascist opposition on members of his local branches. Beckett, in abject disgrace, was ordered back to the BUF's London headquarters, and Moran was exiled to an uncomfortable time in the South Wales mining valleys. Before long, the Tyneside method of dealing with the

Blackshirts was being repeated elsewhere. In June 1934, several thousand anti-fascists "trapped" the Glasgow Fascists in their headquarters, and only police intervention got them out. Those who had set out to shock were now suffering shock.[33]

7: A MESSAGE FROM "BOX 500"

Tyneside's lively drama was inviting the attention of less conspicuous
eyes than those of the main contenders. As one of Britain's main centres
of armaments production, shipbuilding, coal-mining and engineering,
as well as merchant shipping and naval facilities, the North East had an
economic and strategic importance. Moreover, European frictions
coupled with mounting liberation struggles in far-flung colonies such as
the West Indies, India and Palestine, generated a policy of naval and air
force rearmament. In this context, any "subversive" politics readily drew
the curiosity of the state, and particularly if the movements involved
were associated with overseas powers. On these grounds, the
Communist Party had long been a subject of state surveillance, and
Newcastle's postal sorting office at Orchard Street housed a "Home
Office" room where mail addressed to labour organisations and activists
was opened and scrutinised for its political content. Mosley, making no
effort to hide his affinities with Mussolini and Hitler, now joined the list
of those to be watched carefully.

At the Home Office, the ministry responsible for internal security, the
Newcastle and Gateshead street clashes of 13 and 14 May were closely
studied. One reason was that the Home Secretary had to answer a
parliamentary question on 16 May from Jack Lawson, the Labour MP
for Chester-le-Street, echoing the anger of the North East Labour
Movement towards Fascist provocations. Civil servants, in compiling a
response to Lawson, sought reports from the Chief Constables of
Newcastle and Gateshead (each borough then had its own police
force). The Tyneside police had, as it happened, started to review the
nature of BUF activities and the Chief Constable of Gateshead, R. Ogle,
instantly forwarded a file on Tommy Moran's political record. Across
the Tyne, Newcastle's Chief Constable, Frederick Crawley, despatched a
report, heavily marked "Secret", on events in the city on 13 May.
Crawley's Inspector at Cowen's Monument, according to the report,
confirmed that "a number of the Anti-Fascist League or 'grey shirts'
were present" and that about 5000 people – "the more unruly members
of the community" – challenged Beckett. The anti-fascists included
"large numbers of women and boys" who "greeted with cheers" the
arrest of two Blackshirts.

Crawley noted that one of the arrested Fascists, Kenneth Davies, came from London and the other, Charles Bradford, a journalist and "one of the organisers in this area" was bailed by James Pallister of Denton Burn, Newcastle, "an official of the Shell Mex Co." The participation of outsiders like Davies concerned Crawley: "I am informed that a number of B.U.F. 'shock troops' (that is how they were described to me) had been specially sent from London." In this respect, Crawley grasped a salient fact. The Tyneside BUF regularly imported muscle from other parts of the country. Indeed, one former Blackshirt later recollected "a coachload of members" travelling to the North East with the sole intention of "doing over" the local anti-fascists.

The two Blackshirts were charged with fighting and assault. One had struck a constable and the other had attacked two civilians who had gone to the aid of the police. They were fined ten shillings each by the magistrates for fighting and forty shillings for assaulting the police, light penalties at a time when assault charges elsewhere almost always brought imprisonment for anti-fascists.³⁴

Police And Fascism

The BUF was outraged. John Beckett claimed that he had attempted to talk to Crawley about holding a non-provocative meeting, but was afforded an interview only with the deputy Chief Constable. Beckett was scathing about the Newcastle police: "I knew the Chief Constable of Newcastle. His peculiar views and habits had long been a joke in the town." Beckett complained, too, that only three police officers were visible at Cowen's Monument, two on the edge of the vast crowd and "a fat Inspector" who was unwilling to impose order. A.K. Chesterton, one of Mosley's usually less than sober lieutenants according to MI5, even accused the Newcastle police of favouring anti-fascists, unlike in other cities where the police "performed their duties with strict impartiality."

The precise character of Fascist "impartiality" was revealed to Newcastle trade unionist and postal worker, Dave Atkinson, at an unemployed protest procession in Liverpool during this period, which was broken-up by the police with assistance from belt-and-buckle waving Blackshirts! Chesterton was not altogether wide of the mark, however. Police treatment of anti-fascists in Newcastle rarely resulted in charges being laid. Tom Brown of the AFL insisted that "in the Newcastle Bigg

May 25th—31st, 1934.   The Fascist Week   Page 5

TEN FASCISTS ATTACKED BY A THOUSAND REDS

NEWCASTLE POLICE FAIL TO MAINTAIN ORDER

In Absence of Fascist Defence Corps

INDIA AND BRITAIN

A Democratic Constitution Would be Criminal

Fascist Week goes to Wonderland

Market and on the Town Moor…the police were courteous to us." The picture was a little different in Gateshead where anti-fascists had been arrested on 14 May, and a crude attempt had been made to "plant" an offensive weapon on Tom Brown. But much to the chagrin of Chesterton and the Fascist press, the Newcastle police pressured the BUF to stop holding open-air meetings and regarded the Blackshirts as the source of most trouble.[35]

MI5

Crawley urged the Home Office to send his report on to "Box 500", the clandestine address of MI5. By May 1934 the government had committed the secret service to monitoring the BUF's rapid growth. This step had taken a few months to implement because cuts in public expenditure had left MI5 short of staff, and a fine wrangle had taken place behind the scenes over the knotty question of employing a couple of extra clerks. The onset of the new financial year in April 1934 changed the position and, working mainly through provincial Chief

Constables, MI5 began to produce detailed quarterly assessments on "the Fascist Movement in the United Kingdom."

The first report, in June, noted 150 BUF members in Co. Durham (largely at Gateshead, Durham and Darlington) and, in Newcastle upon Tyne, there were thought to be a further 150 "including students of the Armstrong College … mostly young men but only about half take an active part." MI5 observed that Newcastle BUF meetings were "marked by a certain degree of disorder which the Police are inclined to attribute to the aggressiveness of local speakers" and, following the anti-fascist demonstrations of 13 and 14 May, Mosley had ordered a cessation of meetings.

Much intelligence information on the BUF is still shrouded by official secrecy, so it remains hard to evaluate the supposed level of Fascist support. MI5 judged that Fascism was making a considerable impact "in industrial areas" over the first six months of 1934. Possibly taking a cue from secret service informers at the higher levels of English society, the security chiefs also sensed that provincial Chief Constables tended "to underestimate the gravity and importance" of Fascist influence. Against this background, the Director of MI5, Sir Vernon Kell, wrote to Chief Constable Crawley on 9 June 1934 implying unease about the BUF presence in Newcastle, and offering to keep the city's police supplied with Fascist newspapers if they had difficulty obtaining copies locally.[36]

The Newcastle police hardly needed help from MI5's London office to buy a newspaper. Crawley's officers could get the BUF's weekly 'paper from Blackshirts in Newcastle's Northumberland Street on a regular basis (it was even given away free of charge if a potential reader was not prepared to hand over money). Seething with indignation, Crawley penned a stinging reply to Vernon Kell on 12 June telling him not to worry about the Fascists on Tyneside. "Despite the inspired optimism of the Fascists to Newcastle" Crawley wrote, "it would be difficult for the Police to conceive of an area where Fascism is more at variance with the trend of thought of the general public." Crawley had definite ideas about Tyneside "folk" whom he saw as "a hard-headed, matter of fact lot, little inclined to take on strange gods" providing their basic material needs were met. Apart from a few "choice spirits" Fascism appeared "to be a diet of too foreign a brand for this Northern public to assimilate."

352

Box No. 500,

Parliament Street B.O.

SECRET,

London,S.W.1.

96/Northumberland/2/DS/.9b.

9th June, 1934.

Dear Mr. Crawley,

I do not know whether you have seen the "Blackshirt"
for June 1st, 1934, the latest weekly publication of the British
Union of Fascists, but you may be interested in the marked
references in it to fascist activities in your area.

You will notice that it is definitely suggested that the
movement is very active and is making great headway all over the
country.

I should be grateful for your criticism on their view
of the British Union of Fascists activities in your area.

If you have any difficulty in getting further issues of
this paper, would you let me know?

Yours sincerely,

(Sgd). Colonel Sir Vernon Kell.

Secret Home Office papers hint at M15 and Police disagreement (and see opposite)

Officer And Mate

The exchange between MI5 and the Newcastle police exposed a
tension. On the one side was Colonel Sir Vernon George Waldegrave
Kell, the virtual "father" of MI5, a privileged, cut-glass product of the
English Establishment. Kell ran his service with an erudite "light
touch", employing staff drawn from a "military and county" background. By choosing staff so selectively, Kell sought to acquire loyal
agents with private incomes, thereby avoiding the payment of even
moderate salaries.

<u>COPY</u>.   **351**

SECRET.   12th June 1934.
<u>Your Ref</u>: 36/Northumberland/2/DS.9b.

Dear Sir Vernon,

        In reply to yours of yesterday drawing my
attention to a reference to Newcastle in the publication enclosed
of the British Union of Fascists, I beg to state as follows :-

        Despite the inspired optimism of the Fascists to
Newcastle, it would be difficult for Police to conceive of an area
where Fascism is more at variance with the trend of thought of the
general public. The fact is that the folk of the whole of this area
are a hard-headed, matter of fact lot, little inclined to take on
strange gods, providing that food, raiment and shelter are in some
degree obtainable. Of course, there are choice spirits, here as
elsewhere, who will indulge in any effervescence, out of sheer
ennui. At the same time, Fascism does, at the present moment at
all events, appear to be a diet of too foreign a brand for this
Northern public to assimilate.

        I may add that, should Sir Oswald Mosley address
a meeting on the Newcastle Town Moor on Race Sunday, the 24th inst.,
it might very well prove quite a formidable affair. The Newcastle
Fair is said to be the largest in England, and Race Sunday being the

In the Newcastle corner stood a complete contrast in the form of
Frederick Crawley, Chief Constable and former mate of a Cape Horn
barque. Crawley had literally worked his way up from the ranks. Having
gone to sea for a few years around the turn of the century, he joined the

Metropolitan Police prior to the First World War. An early duty was in the Special Branch where he shadowed Bolshevik exiles and came to "know Lenin quite well." Following ten years in the "Met", including two years as a Scotland Yard representative in France, Crawley was appointed Chief Constable of Lincoln. By 1915, he had become the authoritarian Chief Constable of Sunderland (the Home Office wanted "a strong man" for the job), and in 1925 he was appointed chief of the Newcastle police.

Chief Constable Crawley. Photo: John Yearnshire

Crawley was a tough character, and certainly no liberal. He made a reputation by ordering a police baton charge against unemployed workers at Sunderland in 1921, and was not slow to inflict the same treatment on trade unionists in Newcastle during the 1926 General Strike. His distaste for the Fascists stemmed purely from his view that they were troublemakers inspired by foreign ideologies. In this respect, Crawley mirrored his counterpart in Cardiff, where the Mosleyites ran foul of robust policing on occasion, and escaped the accusations of holding BUF sympathies levelled at the Chief Constable of York and both the Manchester and the Metropolitan Police.

Sometimes erratic and unpredictable, and a keen debater of "isms", Crawley was in the opinion of those who knew him, "too free with the rough edge of his tongue for genuine popularity." He lacked "respect for persons" and "made enemies where he could have made friends." But as Kell discovered, Crawley's "unorthodox methods, even though notably successful, did not always commend themselves to Whitehall: and much he cared!" Crawley was renowned for once telling a senior Home Office official "don't try to patronise me." This was not the last the Home Office would hear of Mr. Crawley.[37]

Meanwhile, out on the streets, the "hard headed folk" were having a rare old time.

8: SIR OSWALD ON THE RUN

As MI5 and the Newcastle police privately exchanged brickbats, the politics of Fascism and anti-fascism raged across Tyneside. In a headline-grabbing incident on 1 June 1934, the BUF's Gateshead office at Abbey Terrace was totally wrecked. Apparently, intruders broke into the building whilst the Fascists were away at an Edinburgh rally and inflicted immense damage. Mosley's portrait was "torn into small pieces", mattresses were ripped, gas taps left turned-on and, in the midst of "indescribable confusion", the Blackshirts' Union Jack was stuffed up a chimney. The condition of the premises suggested a possible intention to blow-up Gateshead's Fascist headquarters. Posters had been left behind indicating that the attack was the work of the Greyshirts or Anti-Fascist League.

Newcastle Evening Chronicle, 2 June 1934

A.J. Chater of the AFL strongly denied responsibility, claiming that the raid was really an attempt to discredit the Greyshirts. He may have had a point in the light of MI5's interest. Whatever may have been the case, and the police do not seem to have pursued their investigation very far, the BUF's Gateshead offices had led a precarious existence. Len Edmondson recalled that at one point Jack Cogan of the ILP had led a group of unemployed workers into the BUF offices, chased the Blackshirts away and threatened to set fire to the place; another ILP-er, Barney Molloy, even "brayed the Blackshirts with his belt."[38]

Town Moor Again

The anti-fascists had gained the upper hand since 13 and 14 May, 1934. One consequence of the new situation was reflected in Mosley's handling of his proposed Race Week rally. This mini-Nuremberg display was meant to be a show of strength, flowing from the Beckett-Moran campaign of large meetings. Unable to hold public meetings, the local Blackshirts still busied themselves measuring the Town Moor site and holding rehearsals. The AFL with the North East Federation of Trades Councils, determined to put a stop to Mosley's scheme, announced a counter-demonstration. Anxiety and expectation began to grow, prompting the *Journal* on 11 June to call on Mosley to cancel his rally. By 21 June the *Daily Worker* could report detailed arrangements for the anti-fascist demonstration, including spur marches from Mill Lane in Newcastle's West End, Shields Road in the East End, and Windmill Hills at Gateshead, all joining at the Bigg Market where speakers from trade unions, the ILP and CP would lead a march to the Town Moor. These preparations had an electrifying effect. The Home Office informed Mosley that "counter demon-strations are being organised" and that the Newcastle police could not guarantee the Blackshirts' safety.

Since it was evident that the Fascist rally would be blamed for disorder, Mosley suddenly "postponed" his event, much to the astonishment of the local BUF organiser, Major Ormeston, who heard the decision from the press. The Blackshirts had lost their rally site anyhow because the Race Week amusement and catering operators had simply taken it over for their own uses. In the absence of Mosley, the anti-fascists held a victory march. A large procession "left the Bigg Market" with about 50 Greyshirts in the lead, "carrying banners with stranger devices than Longfellow's 'Excelsior' carrier ever dreamt of."

Trade unionists, peace campaigners and Communists from Chopwell ("Little Moscow"), bearing "well painted cartoons and posters", made their way through the streets to the Town Moor, getting "busy at once, and attested that the cancellation of the Mosley demonstration was due to 'the solidarity of the workers' ... when a young woman with a red beret began to speak they got a great crowd. She trounced the Blackshirts and the National Government with fine impartiality." Just to add to the variety, "the Co-operative Movement had a pitch to defend

Daily Worker, 21 June 1934

their work from Fascist attacks." Mosley, bidding to enrol small shopkeepers, had condemned the Co-ops a month previously.

The Blackshirts were in disarray. Desperate to save face, Mosley announced that he would hold his Town Moor rally after all on 29 July, when the Moor would be empty. Again, the anti-fascists called a counter-demonstration, leafletting factories and streets to rouse support. Chief Constable Crawley, equally resolved to prevent a repeat of the 13/14 May, cancelled all police leave and mobilised 250–400 mounted and foot officers. The Municipal Museum of Science and Industry, overlooking the Moor, was turned into a police communications centre with photographers on the roof and a radio link with a special constable sat in a tree close to where Mosley would speak. This was overkill but it allowed Mosley to hold his meeting backed by Blackshirts transported from as far away as Portsmouth and Plymouth.

)RTH MAIL AND NEWCASTLE CHRONICLE, MONDAY, JULY 30, 1934

SIR O. MOSLEY IN NORTH

INTERRUPTED & HECKLED

BUT NO OUTBREAK OF FIGHTING

WOMEN BANNED

FASCIST LEADER'S PLEA FOR TYNESIDE

SIR OSWALD MOSLEY in a characteristic attitude during his speech at the Fascist rally in

Speaking through six loudspeakers and against the backcloth of a Nazi coup in Austria, Mosley was severely heckled and met "by a volley of small stones and an old dinner fork." Mosley's manner suggested that he was simply going through the motions for the sake of appearances, or just "making his mouth go" to use a graphic Tyneside phrase. Attention was distracted as well by false rumours that news of a joint Italian-Austrian declaration of war against Germany "had been broadcast from London in a special bulletin." After a while, and surrounded by police, the Mosleyites went home, whilst the anti-fascists held a celebratory meeting in the Bigg Market.[39]

North Shields

Prevented from organising in Newcastle and Gateshead, the BUF shifted its emphasis to the Tyne's principal fishing port, North Shields. Tom Hadaway, as a child living in North Shields, saw part of the Fascist campaign:

"I recall the Blackshirts with their lightning flash emblems and banners assembling outside of North Shields railway station, and marching with a drum down to the Harbour View, while we ran alongside expecting to see some trouble. We weren't disappointed.

Tea Parade: Sir Oswald (second from left) inspects the Blackshirts' table manners at a cafe in Newcastle's Haymarket following the July 1934 Town Moor rally. Photo: Newcastle Chronicle & Journal

People said they'd come from Jesmond. I wouldn't know. I'd never been to Jesmond. It may be doing Jesmond a disservice. I remember they looked pretty motley, not like the Jesmond people you see today, and not at all like those crisp uniformed Nazis that appeared on the news reels.

When they arrived at the Harbour View, the heavies cordoned their speaker in the centre, and the local bobbies ringed them again to keep off the crowd. Unfortunately for them the Unemployed Workers Union had its meeting rooms on the corner of Harbour View, and they soon assembled a vigorously hostile crowd of dockside people. Shouts, jeers, pushing and shoving, couldn't hear a word from the speaker, and the general inference was that they should bugga off back to where they came from, or else. There was a kind of charge, and the platform was overwhelmed, the banners got kicked around the square, and the Blackshirts fled in little groups back to the station. I wondered what happened to the drum."

This may have been an incident described by the *Shields News* (12 July 1934) as the "first serious clash" between Fascists and anti-fascists in North Shields, when a 1000-strong crowd including "many women" set the *Blackshirt* paper alight on 11 July 1934. Supporters of the NUWM led by Alec 'Spike' Robson, a well-known Communist seafarer who "collided" with the BUF speaker, drove the Blackshirts off the Harbour View. Robson was arrested and, refusing to be bound-over to keep the peace by "a capitalist court", he was gaoled for a month by the magistrates. He undoubtedly shared the fury of many local unemployed people that the Fascists were presenting James Nichol, one of Robson's neighbours on the Ridges estate (now the Meadowell), as a leader of working class opinion in the town. Apparently, the BUF had recruited Nichol, a former CP branch secretary (a claim repeatedly denied by the Communists), and were using him as a speaker. A further BUF meeting at the Harbour View on 25 July also ended ignominiously when 24 Blackshirts were hounded back to their office by "about 200 children" mercilessly mocking Fascist marching habits![40]

The summer of 1934 seems to have marked a turning point in the advance of the BUF. According to MI5 the Fascists were "losing momentum" over the summer, with a slump in national membership from an estimated 40,000 prior to July down to around 5000 in October. Meetings on Tyneside became rarer and activity on Wearside was negligible. Sales of the *Blackshirt* were "poor" and the numbers of Tyneside branches and members declined in the wake of the formation of the Anti-Fascist League. But if the broad picture was one of retreat, it was perhaps too soon to sustain the claim made in one academic study

Alec 'Spike' Robson in naval uniform. Photo: North Tyneside Trades Union Council

that Newcastle now became an "insignificant" centre for the Fascists. They may have had their problems but, as will be seen, they did not easily give up.[41]

9: FAMOUS FOR FIFTEEN MINUTES

Deprived of easy power and glory, the Mosleyites turned on each other. Rumours of a split in Newcastle Fascism first surfaced in the *North Mail* on 16 August 1934, but it was November before the scale of a vicious internal row emerged from the shadows. At the centre of the bloodletting was Capt. Bruce Norton, the ex-colonial officer, who had angered the BUF's leaders, having been very unpleasant on a coach to a London rally.

Norton's membership of the BUF had been suspended on 16 August, coinciding with evidence of Tyneside activity by a rival Fascist grouping, the rabidly anti-semitic Imperial Fascist League. His sacking sparked about 30 resignations from the Newcastle BUF and, in mid-November, Norton revealed details of the dispute. Alleging that the Newcastle BUF was "threatened with a complete break-up", Norton challenged Major E.W. Ormeston, whom Mosley had instructed to investigate the situation, to " a public debate on Fascism in theory and as practised in the Tyneside area." Norton went on to disclose much about the grubby home life of the BUF. He accused the leaders of operating double-standards, with disciplinary rules applied only to "non-influential" members, whereas no action was taken against officials "guilty of threats towards their own members in cases of internal disputes." Maladministration of Newcastle branch affairs and class discrimination by officers against ordinary Blackshirts had produced not only resignations – "many of whom were original members of the Newcastle organisation" – but, Norton continued: "Newcastle Fascism is no longer Fascism. If this type of administration became national you would have something equivalent to a tyranny." Anti-fascists might have commented that Norton had at last understood the real point of Fascism.

As Norton regaled a meeting of Blackshirt defectors and the local press, the BUF hit back with venom. Ormeston refused to debate with Norton and, instead, issued a statement asserting that the split had been caused by the closure of a canteen, the replacement of an officer and, he hinted darkly, "our determination to wipe out the old 'black gang' impression that people in the Newcastle district seem to have." Yet another former army officer, Major Heads, was drafted in to sort out the mess. These developments were presented to the BUF rank-and-file around the country in a rare admission of divisions when the *Blackshirt*

ICLE,   WEDNESDAY, NOVEMBER 14, 1934 Sunrise, To-morrow, 7.40; lights out, 7.10.   PAGE 7

Threatened Break-Up Of The Newcastle Branch Of Fascists

CAPTAIN B. NORTON RESIGNS

28 OTHERS SAID TO HAVE GIVEN UP MOVEMENT

Newcastle Branch of the British Union of Fascists is threatened with a complete break-up.

CAPTAIN BRUCE NORTON, formerly Area Staff Officer at Newcastle for Northumberland and Durham, has resigned from the movement and he alleges that during the past three months no fewer than 16 male members and 12 women members of the branch have resigned because of their dissatisfaction with its general administration.

He emphasises, however, that he is still a strong adherent of Fascism itself and reveals that he has written to Mr. J. P. Hunter, the officer in charge of the Tyneside area—

Issuing a challenge for a public debate on Fascism in theory and as practised in the Tyneside area, to be held in Newcastle, any time between now and the end of the year.

He is stipulating that those accepting the challenge to debate against him must include one or more of the following:—Captain Norton, Mr. J. P. Hunter, Major Heads (branch officer, Newcastle), Mr. G. C. Simpson (assistant deputy propaganda officer, Newcastle and Leeds) and Mr. J. Theodorson (assistant propaganda officer, Newcastle).

POINTS FOR DEBATE

The principal points upon which he wishes to debate, he also discloses, are:—
(1) Do Fascists believe in law for everybody?
(2) Do they believe in speedy and full investigation of complaints?
(3) Do they believe in all allegations against members being investigated?
(4) Do the rules and regulations issued by national Headquarters in London concern all members or only non-influential ones?
(5) Seeing that Fascism is out to break the use of "influence behind the scenes," should not steps be taken to prevent such influence being used—and abused—in the Fascist ranks themselves?

(6) Is it considered that no action should be taken against members of the British Union of Fascists guilty of throats towards their own members in cases of internal disputes?

The chief grievance which has caused the resignation of so many members, he told a "North Mail" representative yesterday, was that they alleged the officers of the branch broke rules which they themselves had to obey or for having infringed which they were refused admission to the premises.

CAPT. NORTON'S APPOINTMENT

Captain Norton then stated that during the past few years, he confirmed, he had been living in Africa, but in March of this year he became interested in the Fascist movement and came to England to study it.

He reached Newcastle with his wife in April and joined the Newcastle branch of the movement at Clayton Street. He met Mr. John Beckett, formerly M.P. for Gateshead, officer in charge of the National Canvass, who had him appointed immediately as deputy branch officer in charge of the political side of the movement on Tyneside.

Shortly afterwards he met Mr. George G. Vincent, at that time the area administration officer for Yorkshire and the Northern counties. Mr. Vincent took over the whole of the Northern "command" and put Major Ormston in charge of Newcastle as branch officer.

Major Ormston was afterwards appointed as officer in charge of the Northern counties, and Captain Norton was made Area Staff Officer, or second in command under him.

Later, he said, he became involved in a dispute regarding a matter of disciplinary action against another member and an incident in which certain members alleged he had been involved on the way to the Hyde Park meeting in London, and had pressed for full courts of inquiry into these matters.

To his surprise, he was suspended in September and, though he had since pressed for the matter to be investigated, nothing whatever had been done.

Capt. B. NORTON.

INCITEMENT BILL MARCH

THIRD READING IN LORDS

The Incitement to Disaffection Bill was read a third time and passed without division in the House of Lords last night, after several attacks had been made upon it.

Viscount Hailsham, Leader of the House, formally moved the reading.

Lord Ponsonby, Leader of the Opposition, reiterated some of the arguments put forward by opponents of the Bill in committee. "The harsh administration of the measure," he added, "may prove to be far more dangerous than the offensive propaganda which it is ostensibly designed to prevent.

"We think that it is very likely to engender among the members of his Majesty's forces some indignation by the supposition which has been put forward that they need protection, which is another way of saying that their loyalty is under suspicion.

"At a time," he concluded, "when the Government are saying that their task is directed towards recovery and reconstruction, it is deplorable that they should display this nervousness and this peevish apprehension by forcing through a measure which is unpopular."

Lord Strickland maintained that the Socialists knew perfectly well that if they did not administer this measure with stringency their enemies the Fascists would very soon take their places. He regarded the opposition to the Bill as political propaganda which was not sup-

---

PERTS ER

he estimates by ars to a 1926 ome amusement County Court

t Helen Street, er, claimed £26 Thomas Blake, Newcastle, a for repairs to ch had been lorry.

, plaintiff estimated £19, while an e said that 30s.

re judgment for r replacement of a respect of loss and garage fees

---

are Of Plot

NEY-GENERAL

(Soc., Glasgow, Attorney General mons yesterday,

North Mail & Newcastle Daily Chronicle, 14 November 1934

reported that Heads had "the backing of the whole membership, and they pay tribute to the magnificent manner he had handled the situation of purging the branch of unwanted and undesirable members."

However, the BUF's unsavoury reputation of enrolling "the corner-ends" could not be so readily shaken off. Two Blackshirts were arrested in Newcastle's Gosforth area for "drunkenness" after they stole eleven bottles of beer and 6s 5d from the Gateshead BUF office in October 1934. Shortly afterwards, the secretary of the BUF's Shields Road branch in Newcastle's East End was convicted of house-breaking.[42]

Blackshirt Women

Grand impressions of "intense activity" on Tyneside were given by the Fascist press following Heads's appointment, but were intended to conceal the true picture. The Norton squabble had its casualties, including the BUF's women's section. The *Blackshirt* had made a great deal of the opening of a women's branch at Gateshead in October, stemming from the recruitment of a Conservative Party official, Jean Cossar, who had held several Tory organising posts since 1923. Cossar joined the Newcastle BUF in the autumn of 1934 and threw herself into promoting Fascism, setting up women's groups at Gateshead and South Shields. The initiative was shortlived.

The BUF was hampered by its ambiguous attitude towards women. Within the movement there was a continuing tension over the proper role of women. Some Fascists favoured a limited equality, but most agreed with Mosley that politically alert women were not "normal". In any event, Tyneside had its own problems. Mrs. Norton said on 17 November that the local Fascist women's organisation "had been practically wiped out as a

result of the dispute" involving her husband. The shattering of the
women's organisation was also confirmed by Lady Mosley in a conversa-
tion monitored by the Special Branch in January 1935. She complained
that a BUF national officer, Major A. Gleghorn, "insulted some of their
best people" and especially the women when visiting the North East,
resulting in further resignations and the prospect of branch closures.

More bluntly, a Newcastle clerk, George Cameron Simpson, who had
quit the BUF, wrote to Mosley in January 1935: "Your movement is
smashing up in the North through bad management."[43]

A Revival Attempted

Gripped by a crisis rooted in the strength of the anti-fascist campaign of
May-June 1934, and reinforced by very bad publicity in the aftermath of
Blackshirt savagery at a huge rally at Olympia in London together with
Mosley's loss of the *Daily Mail*'s support, Fascism on the Tyne and the
Wear was rapidly slipping into oblivion. Sufficient resilience and money
remained, however, enabling the BUF to try to resume momentum.
Vincent Collier was sent back to the North East in February 1935 to
mastermind a revival. Under Collier's direction, meetings were staged
in the mining villages around Trimdon, Co. Durham, and at Sunderland, South Shields, Durham, Washington, Benwell and Felling as well
as in Northumberland. Hilda Ashby, who grew up in Chopwell, remembered that "in 1935, the Blackshirts came out to hold an open-air
meeting" at the village's Hotel Corner, but were stopped by "the local
Labour lads" who occupied the meeting place.

Usually, these meetings were quick "hit and run" episodes, avoiding the
possibility of opposition, except at Newcastle's Bigg Market where
Collier and friends tended to get hit before they could run. Typical of
this phase was a meeting reported by the *Journal* (26 March 1935):
"After considerable inactivity in outdoor speaking in the centre of
Newcastle, Fascists held a meeting in Newcastle Bigg Market last night
... [The speakers] had a hostile reception, and the meeting closed to a
storm of booing and shouting."

The public face of the BUF was only part of the story. There were
people who actively sympathised with the Fascists but, for their own

reasons, did so with circumspection. In 1990, "A Newcastle Old Blackshirt", writing in the Mosleyite newsletter *Comrade*, drew attention to a BUF undercover man, Tommy Hastings. Apparently, Hastings was employed in the Customs and Excise and, as a Newcastle "convert" to the BUF in 1935, did not enrol as a formal member so as to protect his job. On the other hand, Hastings took all the BUF journals, "often buying extra copies" to distribute in an unspecified way. This revelation poses the intriguing question of how many more secretive Fascists may have been present on the Tyne and the Wear during the late-thirties?

City Hall

A feature of the Blackshirts' dispiriting revival effort in the spring of 1935 was another appearance from Mosley. Newcastle now represented something of a challenge for Mosley. The wild events of 1934 still struck a chord at the beginning of 1935, not least because Mosley had become embroiled in a libel action against John Marchbanks, general secretary of the National Union of Railwaymen. Marchbanks, "encouraged by the stand taken by Newcastle people in preventing Mosley appearing on the Town Moor" in June 1934, had delivered a speech at Newcastle alleging that the Fascists were planning to overthrow democracy by armed force. Denying the charge, Mosley took the matter to court in January 1935. Although he won, the jury made a telling point by awarding him damages of only one farthing and no costs.

Not wishing to revisit the Town Moor and provide a focus for the anti-fascists, the BUF hired the City Hall from Newcastle's right-wing city council for a rally on 26 May. Len Edmondson retained a keen memory of the occasion:

> "Before the Mosley meeting, anti-fascist propaganda was being circulated. A Workers' Bookshop on Westgate Road, which I believe was run by the Communist Party, published an anti-fascist news sheet on the Friday before the meeting. This was a single-page broadsheet called *Mosley Unmasked*",

and was sold on the streets. On the night of the Mosley rally, Len Edmondson was at another meeting in the ILP's Westfield Hall:

"Then, suddenly, a man burst into the Hall and said Mosley's meeting had been smashed up after only 15 minutes. He had been howled down by the City Hall audience. Every time he rose to speak he was drowned out. I don't think there was any violence ... The large numbers of anti-fascists made the Blackshirts powerless to do anything. Mosley had to close the meeting."

A good deal of the opposition to Mosley among the 2000-strong City Hall audience was, in Len Edmondson's judgement, "spontaneous" rather than organised. The Anti-Fascist League seems to have dissolved by May 1935, and organised anti-fascism had once more become the province of small political parties such as the CP, the ILP, branches of the Socialist League at Gateshead, Wallsend and Newcastle, or interested trade unionists and members of the NUWM. Nevertheless, popular antagonism towards Fascism was now well-entrenched.

The *Journal* confirmed the nature of the City Hall meeting. Mosley was "howled down", accused of "Hitlerism" and using "thugs", and "after a barrage of interruptions he closed the meeting abruptly and walked off the platform amid a demonstration of hostility." As he disappeared "the opposition cheered vociferously." It had all been over in just 15 minutes from start to finish. Leaving the Hall, Mosley was escorted back to the BUF's Lovaine Street offices by mounted police and 200 imported Blackshirts. "Great interest" was shown in the procession by "the public", some of whom threw more than insults.[44]

Mosley And The Police

Mosley was furious. Sympathy came from the *Daily Express* but Fascism had totally failed to carry a triumph on Tyneside yet again. Once more the BUF blamed the Newcastle police for letting them down. The *Blackshirt* accused the police of protecting "the Reds" at the City Hall and "apparently acting under orders, stood by impotently" whilst inhibiting the Blackshirt stewards: "The Police were rewarded with a nice round of applause from the Reds." Mosley wrote to Richard Embleton, chairman of the Newcastle watch committee, and Chief Constable Crawley's employer, calling for a public inquiry into the policing of the City Hall. Embleton merely replied that order at an indoor meeting was the responsibility of the organisers and the police had not detected any breach of the peace which could have persuaded them to intervene.

The BLACKSHIRT, May 31, 1935

LARGEST CIRCULATION AMONG POLITICAL WEEKLIES

FREE OFFER TO ADVERTISERS
See Page 3

FREE OFFER TO SUBSCRIBERS
See Page 3

Blackshirt
INCORPORATING
THE FASCIST WEEK

THE ONLY FASCIST WEEKLY NEWSPAPER

No. 110. MAY 31st, 1935   BRITAIN FIRST   (Registered at G.P.O. as a Newspaper)   ONE PENNY

GOVERNMENT PROTECT RED HOOLIGAN!
POLICE FAIL TO PRESERVE ORDER AT NEWCASTL|

STEWARDS THREATENED WITH ARREST

NEW PHASE OF PARLIAMENTARY DECADENCE

An organised attempt was made by Communists to break up the Newcastle City Hall meeting which succeeded, with the protection of the police, who are subject to Government control. The following manifesto was issued before the meetings:—

"Demonstrate against Mosley on May 26.
"On Sunday, May 26, Mosley will endeavour to put forward his Fascist policy in the Newcastle City Hall, supported by his Blackshirt gangsters.
"Whenever he gets away with a Blackshirt rally all the forces of reaction are directly encouraged.
"This is no question of ordinary Party politics and discussion, but the menace

FAREWELL TO RAMSAY?

HISTORY WILL ACCOUNT HIM A GREAT FAILURE

Speculation on the end of the present MacDonald Administration draws upon imagination (and the gossip of the lobbies) to fill in the details, but the broad outlines of Governmental changes are now well known.

The outstanding change, at the moment of going to press, seems to be that Mr. MacDonald feels unable to continue in the Premiership, and, unless the plan is subjected to modification at the last moment, Mr. Baldwin once more will be the Prime Minister.

When we remember the performances of Mr. Baldwin in the past when he was in

In fact, the Inspector in charge at the City Hall had intervened in the conduct of the meeting .... but to prevent Blackshirt stewards from throwing out anti-fascist hecklers! This incident unleashed a further colourful exchange between Crawley and his critics at the Home Office. Previously secret Home Office files record MI5 interest in the City Hall rally and an acrimonious correspondence between civil servants and Crawley. The Home Office told the Chief Constable on 8 June that the Newcastle police should have assisted the Blackshirts and the Inspector on duty was "ill-advised" in his decision. Crawley, as usual, marshalled his own robust version of events. He had deployed 150 officers around the Hall, knowing that a Communist meeting in the Bigg Market had resolved to go to the City Hall, and that "a considerable number of Communists and unemployed were in position in the Hall."

The police impression, Crawley informed the Home Office, was that Mosley was largely to blame for what happened, and had even created the situation to prove that the police could not keep order at his rallies ("Mosley virtually confided this to me prior to the meeting"). An open meeting, wrote Crawley, "invites disturbers" and particularly "in the case of a novel, perhaps foreign brand of politics." Mosley's "peculiar style" of clothing and manner "are definitely provocative to North country types, including a large number of unemployed in this distressed area." A "considerable proportion" of the audience were hostile to Mosley and the Inspector therefore prevented the stewards from ejecting people because "such action might then have provoked a breach of the peace." The Home Office remained unimpressed.[45]

Mosley held another meeting at the City Hall on 6 November 1935. Repeating his Town Moor tactics, he relied upon loudspeakers to match severe heckling, but the meeting disintegrated when "pandemonium broke loose" as Blackshirts tried to remove anti-fascists. This rally was part of a BUF revival campaign launched in the wake of Mosley's 15-minutes fiasco. The seemingly inexhaustible pool of ex-army officers was dredged again to produce Capt. S.C. Crossley, whose mission was one of "reorganising" the Newcastle BUF. There came some debates with young Tories at Newcastle and elsewhere – firmly declared "unofficial" by the Newcastle Conservative Association – and meetings with Collier as speaker were claimed at Trimdon, Wallsend, Durham, Byker and Chester-le-Street over the summer and autumn.

Blackshirt Baiting

Anti-fascists repeatedly broke up Collier's meetings at the Bigg Market, described by the *Blackshirt* as the "happy hunting ground of the opponents of Fascism." Tom Callaghan, venturing to Bigg Market political meetings as a young boy, noticed that there "was always one event that brought the Communists and the majority of their critics together. This was the arrival of Oswald Mosley's Blackshirts! Dressed in black shirts, black trousers and boots, and wide leather belts, they looked an unsavoury lot as they formed themselves around their platform ... their political Messiah was Adolf Hitler. I gave them up, they were neither interesting or entertaining ... I felt certain that

without [a police presence] the Blackshirts would have been chased out
of the market-place by their many opponents."

The Way to Knock Out Fascism and War

New Leader, 1935

At Benwell, in Newcastle's West End, Tom Callaghan and other
children were preparing on one occasion to hurl clods of earth at the
Blackshirts when mayhem broke out:

"We all sprang up on the wall in time to witness that the meeting
was being broken-up in a frantic free-for-all. The speaker had been
pulled down off his platform, and his bodyguard were in complete
disarray. Despite the presence of the Police who were struggling to
separate the two groups of antagonists, the superior number of
anti-fascists coupled with their obvious united fury and determination, proved too much for those who were doing their utmost
to resist, and the Police were forced temporarily to retreat, and the
Blackshirts were chased out of sight!"

Only with heavy police protection could the Blackshirts later hold a march along Benwell's Adelaide Terrace.[46]

Collier, meanwhile, fared worse at Sunniside, Sunderland, where 400 anti-fascist miners knocked him off his speaker's box in July. Sunderland consistently offered Fascist speakers a suicidal experience and on 8 October the BUF claimed that Collier was embattled by "500 people who had abandoned a Friends of the Soviet Union meeting and who were determined to smash the Blackshirt meeting."

Many of the members take no active part. The class of persons frequenting the two local branches are very mixed, a number being of the better class, others of the working class, and "lodging house" type. The Secretary of the Shields Road branch was recently convicted of house-breaking. There has been a considerable increase of activity in the last few weeks, more than the normal number of meetings being held in connection with the Italo-Abyssinian campaign.

Social attitudes show in a secret report on the Newcastle BUF prepared for M15 by Chief Constable Crawley in 1935

Crossley and Collier proved unable to salvage Fascism's prospects. To some extent, their efforts were negated by another BUF internal conflict, this time over the status of uniformed Fascists. A Special Branch report to the Home Office/MI5 monitors in October 1935 disclosed that Crossley made "no secret of his hostility to the Blackshirt organisation", preferring to present the BUF as a conventional political party. In any event, the Special Branch concluded that Newcastle Fascism was "in a very chaotic state." The MI5 reports for 1935 suggested that despite a considerable BUF financial input – the Newcastle District was annually receiving £100 as payment of office rents and £200 for organisers' salaries – the membership was fluctuating between 60–150 people, with "many taking no active part." The "class of persons frequenting the two local branches", wrote Chief Constable Crawley in characteristic patronising tone, was believed to be "very mixed", embracing "a number of the better class, others of the working class, and 'lodging house' type." Towards the close of 1935 the BUF announced one more "reorganisation" in the North East.[47]

10 : LORD HAW HAW

Richard Kelly, a renowned journalist, has a student tale of the mid-1930s: "As Chairman of the student Socialist Society, I attended a Newcastle Fascist meeting in a building next door to the Union then called the Assembly Rooms. It was addressed by William Joyce who told me to 'shut my beautiful mouth' after which I was ejected with many others." William Joyce, who later became "Lord Haw Haw", the wartime radio voice of Nazi Germany, took more than a passing interest in the Tyne and the Wear.

Joyce was in at the beginning of the nightmare. From time to time he was active in the Conservative Party, but he had been a member of the British Fascisti in the 1920s as well. When Mosley's BUF was formed, Joyce enrolled and was soon touring the North East. His first recorded visit was on 9 January 1934 when he addressed "a moderate attendance" at the Hetton Miners' Hall, attacking democracy, advocating dictatorship and eulogising Hitler. The following December, "Professor William Joyce" (he claimed some academic distinction) was at the Durham BUF offering to end class war with a strong dose of Fascist violence. Thereafter, as deputy leader of the BUF, he travelled to Tyneside frequently and could be found battling with a "Red Flag" singing audience at South Shields in May 1935.

At South Shields, Joyce secured a hearing only with the help of a female Tory Party official but was then put on the defensive by a Jewish heckler, the ultimate indignity for a raving anti-semite. Undaunted, Joyce went on to speak "at a luncheon to a group of Tyneside businessmen", then to the Grand Assembly Rooms, Newcastle, where the "hecklers were in good form" and Richard Kelly and friends told him to go to Italy.[48]

Italy, as it happened, was far from William Joyce's mind. His views of Mussolini's Fascism were dismissive in the extreme, since Joyce regarded Italians as racially inferior to Nordic races. Joyce, at this time, was angling for cash from his real heroes, the German Nazis. In August, he sent a lengthy, confidential report on the BUF to Otto Bene, the head of the Nazi network in Britain. The report was shot through with exaggerations, including Joyce's description of Mosley's fifteen minutes fiasco at the Newcastle City Hall in May:

William Joyce, The Blackshirt, 17 May 1935

MR. JOYCE ON TYNESIDE

The Director of Propaganda, Mr. William Joyce, has returned from his visit to Tyneside. On Thursday last he addressed a well-attended meeting at South Shields. Organised opposition was unsuccessfully attempted; and after the meeting very many members of the audience came to congratulate the speaker on the success of the meeting.

On the following day Mr. Joyce spoke at a luncheon to a group of Tyneside business men. In the evening he addressed a public meeting at the Barras Bridge Assembly Rooms.

The meeting was well attended and in every way satisfactory. The opposition was present; but, on the advice of the stewards, the would-be interrupters decided to be silent. The speech was received with frequent applause, some time was spent in answering questions; and, after the National Anthem had been very cordially sung, Mr. Joyce addressed the members who had attended the meeting.

NOW THAT YOU *!*
UNDERSTAND *!*

HELP TO ESTABLISH THIS NEW VIRILE FORM OF GOVERNMENT

POST THIS FORM TO NEAREST BRANCH
OR TO
**BRITISH UNION OF FASCISTS
SLOANE SQ., LONDON, S.W.3**

NAME...

ADDRESS..

....

....

I wish to become an $\frac{ACTIVE}{NON\text{-}ACTIVE}$ Member of The British Union of Fascists.
Please forward the necessary forms, etc.

"At a meeting held recently in Newcastle-on-Tyne, a great Industrial centre, organised Red interruption was carried out under Police protection. As the B.U.F does not propose to enter into conflict with the law, the meeting was abandoned, to the intense indignation of the public, who lined the roads and gave the Fascist salute to the Fascists as they marched away from the hall where the meeting was held."

Joyce alleged that the Newcastle police had acted on political instructions in their handling of the meeting. It was a point that may have puzzled the Home Office, emerging from a bracing encounter with Chief Constable Crawley, as its officials read Joyce's report: MI5 had obtained a copy almost as quickly as Otto Bene! The Nazi leaders in Berlin also found the report interesting but apparently declined to part with their Reichsmarks.[49]

George Hardy, who was employed at the Newcastle Workers' Bookshop during the mid-1930s, recounted in his autobiography, *Those Stormy Years*, details of one of Joyce's wilder visits:

"Soon after I began to work in Newcastle, a loudspeaker van came one Saturday morning along Westgate Road, announcing that Captain Joyce would speak on the Town Moor on the afternoon of the following day. I said to Charlie Woods, the [Communist Party] district secretary, 'Could we stop him?' We had just 24 hours to do it. We got out a leaflet – it must have been the briefest I ever drafted – and it just said: 'Attention, Attention!' gave the time and place of the Mosleyite meeting and wound up with the words: 'Fascists should not be allowed to speak in Newcastle.' We had it printed in time to hand out to the Saturday night crowds. Next day, at 3 p.m., about 800 people turned up at the Town Moor. They began singing soon after Joyce started. He couldn't make himself heard, even over the microphone, and he retaliated by singing 'God Save the King.' Then the crowd roared 'Rat!' and sang louder than ever. Joyce had to pack up.

The Geordies were the victors. It was the last time, I believe, that this traitor's voice was heard in Newcastle until he started snarling at us as Lord Haw Haw over the Nazi radio stations early in the war."

There was one arrest at Joyce's meeting. Thomas Richardson, a Houghton-le-Spring miner, was fined £1 for "disorderly conduct", amounting to heckling Joyce at the Town Moor on 1 September 1935 with the words: "Down with Fascism!" Other people were less restrained and "several hundred persons, many, judging by their frequent interruptions, being in the hostile camp" kept up a barrage of songs such as 'The Internationale" and "The Red Flag". Joyce and his Blackshirts, in Len Edmondson's words, were "pelted" with stones on their way to and from the Moor. One lifelong Fascist, John Charnley, recruited by Tommy Moran and who subsequently claimed to have had invitations to Buckingham Palace Garden parties and to have shared a platform with Michael Heseltine, always remembered that "Town Moor, Newcastle, was rough." William Joyce did return to the North

East after his Town Moor set-back, but only to poorly attended BUF meetings at Hexham and South Shields early in 1936.[50]

Anti-Semitism

Joyce's appearances underlined Fascism's anti-semitism and racism. German Fascists resident in the North East or connected with the area had eagerly displayed their prejudices in the letter columns of the local press. In April 1933, the *Sunderland Echo* published a pro-Nazi, anti-Jewish letter from Dr. P. Berens of Koln-Ehrenfeld who had taught at Bede School in 1930–31. A month later, a German Pastor at the South Shields Seamen's Mission was condemning the Bishop of Durham's opposition to anti-semitism and defending Hitlerism. Others regularly followed suit, including a Dr. H.G. Telle of Berlin University, and resident in Newcastle for a year, who argued in favour of curbs on German liberty as a result of "the Jewish problem" before a meeting of the Tyneside League of Nations Union in 1936.

Although a broad span of opinion rejected anti-semitism, there were those in the North East who did exhibit hostility towards Jewish people. A furore was generated in December 1933 when members of the middle-class Middlesbrough and District Motor Club voted to ban any further membership applications from Jews. Six Jewish members resigned in protest and the subsequent row reverberated around newspaper correspondence columns and pubs. By and large, the Club's decision was roundly condemned by the region's principal newspapers such as *The Northern Echo*.

The BUF's own anti-semitism became more pronounced as time went on. Tom Callaghan recalled a Blackshirt speaker in Benwell around 1935 "informing his audience, how Germany, was solving its unemployment problem. And then, for what appeared to me at that moment, an unrelated deviation; he began letting loose an obviously worked-up venom towards Jews ... he appeared to froth at the mouth whenever he mentioned ... these alleged enemies of his. Soon I gathered that in essence, the whole of his remarks on the evils of unemployment, and the cause of it, amounted to the blame being directly attributed to the curtailment of capital investment by the Jews." Quite apart from the bigotry upon which the BUF's anti-semitism was

THE NORTHERN ECHO, WEDNESDAY, 20 DECEMBER, 1933.

AN UNFORTUNATE TRIAL RUN.   By PIP.

" Drat it, this can't be doing the old bus any good!"

based, the Fascist claims flew in the face of facts. Jewish refugees from Germany and Central Europe were to the fore in opening new factories in North Shields and on Tyneside trading estates during the depressed 1930s, directly contributing towards the creation of employment.[51]

No amount of job creation by Jewish refugees could appease the Fascists, of course. Jewish property in Gateshead suffered attacks, with damage and anti-semitic slogans at the Bensham synagogue twice in July 1935. Vincent Collier ranted at Sunderland's West Sunniside in late-July "that opposition to the Fascists in Britain was financed by the Jews", and this dreary tale was repeated more than once. Widespread anti-semitism was a dismal feature of the period and seen by the BUF as an opportunity. Letters to the *Shieldsman* in 1935 attacked Tynemouth Labour Party for selecting "a Russian Jew" as their parliamentary candidate, and the Newcastle Society of Jewish Ex-Servicemen was prevented from criticising the British Legion's "friendly overtures" to Germany by Sir Arthur Lambert, when he chaired the annual meeting of Legion's Newcastle Central branch in November 1935. At South Shields, as David Clark, MP, noted in his history of the town's Labour

Party, *We Do Not Want The Earth,* Labour activists were acutely aware of anti-semitism among influential civic leaders in the 'thirties.

"I wasn't too politically conscious – most people of my age weren't really politically conscious – but I remember Mosley and his Black Shirts vividly. The ones that I saw on Tyneside around Mosley at his meetings were known for what they were – they were a lot of villains. I heard him speaking but I wasn't influenced by him at all. What I didn't like was, and I was involved in this in the city one day, I saw two Black Shirts giving a Jew in Blackett Street a hammering and of course I was young and I was fit and I jumped in, and I would do the same today if I saw two of the Black Shirts or two of the National Front assaulting somebody – I'd feel duty bound to go to that person's assistance. I was incensed that day because I'd seen it for the first time with my own eyes. Now that was the Black Shirts attitude to the man who was born a Jew – I mean 'there but for the grace of God...' it could have been us, we could have been born a Jew just the same way. I thought that there's something basically wrong with this political party and I could never have thought of supporting it."

Terence Monaghan in Keith Armstrong and Huw Beynon, *Hello, Are You Working?* (Strong Words, Whitley Bay, 1977)

Albert Gompertz

A fair slice of anti-semitism in South Shields was directed against a remarkable character named Albert Gompertz, teetotaller, vegetarian, conscientious objector in the First World War, and son of Dutch Jewish parents. Gompertz was also an ardent Socialist and shop workers' trade unionist. As secretary of South Shields Labour Party and a Labour councillor, he conducted a vigorous opposition to the business elite controlling the council (obstructing, for example, their attempts to offer council contracts to German Nazi firms in 1934). He was removed from the council chamber on no less than three occasions by the police, acting on the instructions of irate mayors during the 1930s. Conscious of the unfairness of discrimination, Gompertz gave a good deal of support to fighting for civil rights for Shields' Arab population.[52]

Gompertz's enemies looked for ways of getting their revenge on their far too effective opponent. A chance arose in March 1934 when Gompertz was holding one of his regular Labour open-air meetings in Shields Market Place. A senior police officer was sent to stop the meeting and arrested Gompertz for disturbing the peace. "The incident" as David Clark observed, "provided just a hint of anti-semitism among the establishment of the town." At the time, the South Shields Labour Party firmly contested Gompertz's arrest, rightly seeing the affair as an attack on freedom of speech. Much to the discomfort of the police and the municipal leaders, Gompertz won and the charge against him was dismissed. But this was not the only curious case of its kind. In October 1935, the town's magistrates threw out a further charge brought by the police against a Communist for selling newspapers unlawfully. During the court hearing it became apparent that the police had been quite happy to allow Fascists to sell the *Blackshirt* but had singled out anti-fascists for arrest.

The stand taken by Albert Gompertz was grounded in the strong anti-fascist resolve of the South Shields Labour Party and Trades Council, which opposed Fascism from its re-emergence in the area. When Austrian Socialists were killed fighting an extreme right-wing dictatorship in February 1934, the party and the trades council noted "the gallant stand our Austrian comrades had made against fascism, bearing witness to Socialism with their lives." This was followed by a Labour anti-fascist meeting in Shields Market Place.

The Labour Party and Gompertz were concerned, too, about the presence in April 1934 of Wilhelm Hacker "a German Fascist operating in South Shields." Hacker was a 34-years old German sailor with the bizarre habit of giving Heil Hitler salutes in the streets. The town's magistrates ordered Hacker to keep the peace after one street incident in June 1934, and then imprisoned him for a month following a disturbance in July. Gompertz pressed for Hacker's deportation, pointing out that the government was allowing a disruptive Nazi sympathiser to remain in England whilst barring entry to German refugee democrats.[53]

47

campaign. (3) that upon certain information being conveyed to the Secretary the line of action now agreed upon be carried out.

Meeting against ft. fascist tyranny.

It was agreed that an outdoor meeting in the Market Place be arranged to enter our Protest & horror against the Austrian Governments treatment of Socialists & our own determination to resist Fascism & Tyranny.

Alexander Stephenson *Signed* (Chairman

MEETING of the TRADES Council held February 20. Comrade A. Stephenson in the chair.

Austrian Socialists fight for Freedom.

The chairman made reference to the gallant stand our Austrian Comrades had made against fascism bearing witness to Socialism with their lives, the delegates paid tribute to their memory by standing in silence —————

Minutes

MINUTES of MEETING held February 6. read & confirmed MINUTES of Executive Committee held February 16. —————— read & adapted —————

The Memorial to Parliament by the London and Manchester Trades Councils was endorsed. Councillor W. PEARSON moved the following Resolution

South Shields Trades Council & Labour Party Minutes, February 1934

South Shields

The anti-fascist solidarity and internationalism of the Shields labour movement produced some striking displays in the autumn of 1935. Against the background of Mussolini's invasion of Abyssinia, and renewed BUF activity in South Shields, a vast 6000-strong anti-fascist procession took place on 8 September. The core of the procession was provided by 2000 Bolden Colliery miners and their band together with over 200 members of the Co-operative Women's Guild and the Bolden Colliery Labour Women's Section. Women were accorded pride of place as the column wound its way from Bolden to Shields. On the way they were joined by groups from churches and chapels as well as members of miners' lodges at Harton and Whitburn "with their band and banner." The South Shields Communist Party "with a huge red flag" also took part. At a great rally in front of the Old Town Hall, the crowd approved a resolution demanding that the British government support League of Nations action to "cancel out the dual brutes, Fascism and War."

A few days prior to the anti-fascist rally, Vincent Collier, sheltering behind a protective cordon of Shields police, had been forcefully heckled in the Market Place by "a coloured man" wearing army medals who took the Fascist propaganda apart. This was a poignant development because the BUF was promoting racial hatred against the black and Arab communities produced by Shields' seafaring traditions. There had been serious racial violence between Arab and white sailors at Shields in 1919, and a further clash had occurred in 1930 during a seafarers' strike. Mosley, on his visits to Tyneside, had called for the exclusion of black sailors from British ships and this fitted with the strikebreaking tactics of the shipowners and the corrupt leadership of the National Union of Seamen.

But the Fascists had misjudged the mood in Shields. The 1930 "riot" at the Mill Dam had not been primarily a racial disturbance. Instead, there had been contrived provocation and violence by "scabs" and the police. This action was directed against Arab sailors with the intention of breaking a united front mounted by black and white workers seeking to improve employment conditions. The stark assault on the Arabs, and the subsequent hardship they experienced, contributed to an attitude change already under way in Shields. Gradually and quietly an under-

DEMONSTRATION AGAINST WAR AND FASCISM

The procession, with banners, arriving in South Shields Market Place last night for the mass demonstration against War and Fascism.

Photo: *Shields Gazette, 9 September 1935*

standing had been growing between Arab and white working-class neighbours reflecting, as Barry Carr has written in *Black Geordies*, his penetrating study of the Shields Arabs, how "the whole ethos of Tyneside working-class culture was anathema to the bullying on which racism is built."

Perhaps nothing gave a practical edge to the atmosphere in Shields more than the reaction to Mosley's blatant attempt at incitement on 3 November 1935. The Fascists arranged a meeting to be addressed by Mosley at the Palace Cinema, located near to the town's "Arab quarter". Over 150 Blackshirt stewards were pulled in "from Leeds, London, Liverpool and Newcastle" for what the *North Mail* described as "one of the most remarkable meetings ever held in South Shields." If Mosley had been confident of instigating a pogrom against the Arabs, he was to be severely disabused. As the meeting commenced, with "thousands of people" outside the cinema, "the uproar was terrific." Fights broke out between Blackshirts and hecklers, leading to a mass walkout from the auditorium. The Blackshirts soon beat a retreat, some being chased away and others in buses "subjected to a shower of stones."

The failure to spark a race riot at Shields was an inglorious end to the BUF's autumn campaign. One of Collier's meetings at Sunderland had been closed by the police in September as anti-fascists marched towards his platform. And just prior to Mosley's South Shields humiliation, "a bunch of children" had virtually seen off a Blackshirt meeting at Byker in Newcastle.[54] From Byker to North Shields, the Fascists were evidently no match for the Geordie kids!

11 : FROM BOSTON TO MADRID

The world was careering towards war. Across Africa, Asia and Europe, Fascism grew more aggressive, greedily demanding more territory. Fascist ambitions were insatiable and, in July 1936, these exploded in Spain when army generals revolted against the elected government of the Spanish Republic. It quickly emerged that the uprising was Fascist in flavour and its leader, General Franco, enjoyed no shortage of help from Hitler and Mussolini. But the Republic, assisted by the Spanish labour movement, fought back against those who plotted to destroy democracy.

Anti-fascists at once grasped the dangers posed by a Fascist victory in Spain. Not only might Fascism stifle a hard-won democracy, but the civil war unfolding in Spain would serve as an armed rehearsal for Nazi designs elsewhere. This was why the Spanish Republic became such a major cause for anti-fascism, inspiring countrywide solidarity campaigns and enormous personal sacrifices. As early as September 1936 the ILP was instrumental in convening a Newcastle conference involving Labour Party, trade union, Co-operative and Socialist League organisations to promote aid for Spain. This quickly led to a rally at the city's Palace Theatre on 14 September, attended by about 3000 people and organised by the Communist Party.

Establishing unity in support of the Spanish Republic was not always an easy task. The national leaderships of the Labour Party and the Trades Union Congress ruled out joint projects involving Communists and other left-wingers, and the TUC's *Daily Herald* strongly advocated non-intervention in Spain. At the same time, Roman Catholicism, pitted against the anti-clerical Republic, contained a body of pro-Franco opinion which made its influence felt in labour politics at local levels. These two elements could produce a degree of inertia. Jim Fyrth, in his history of the Aid for Spain Movement noted that in "Newcastle and the North East, the Labour Party and many unions hesitated to throw their support into the Spain campaign, so that unofficial committees with rather narrower aims conducted the work." But, as in the struggle against the Blackshirts, many Labour activists simply ignored national directives and got on with the job, working with whoever showed an interest. Human sympathy for the victims of Franco's brutality and deep commitments to anti-fascism were the spurs to action.

Aid For Spain

Part of the solidarity effort on the Tyne and the Wear went towards the national campaign to provide food and medical aid for Spain. Much work was underway by 1937, largely organised through a special shop near to the Workers' Bookshop on Newcastle's Westgate Road. Members of the NUWM, hunger marchers, unemployed miners, political parties, all raised money and materials to stock foodships for Spain. Wallsend Labour Party was fairly typical in forming a Spanish Aid Committee in February 1937. Sharing in another national initiative, Voluntary Industrial Aid supported by the Amalgamated Engineering Union, Tyneside engineers, led by workers at Vickers-Armstrong's Elswick factory, "gave up their spare time to recondition old motor-cycle combinations as ambulances for the Spanish people." And over the Tyne, Gateshead anti-fascists, utilising the old device of requisitioning a Town Meeting, committed the borough's mayor to setting-up a Spanish Relief and Medical Aid Fund in April 1937.

Despite the poverty and unemployment afflicting Tyneside throughout the 1930s, the aid for Spain campaigns galvanised a level of generosity made all the more splendid because those who gave the most generally had the least to give. Hilda Ashby, at unemployment-stricken Chopwell, for instance, recalled that "we collected loads of food in 1936. We had women making bandages and sheets for Spain." This outburst of humanity enabled Tyneside to send its own foodship to Spain in 1938, following a tremendous public appeal attracting widespread support. And one of the key advocates of the foodship was Michael Weaver, the Conservative parliamentary candidate for Workington. Weaver, like some other Tories, visited Spain as a sympathiser of the generals and their revolt but, horrified by the reality, returned to England determined to maintain the Republic.

A principal instigator of Aid for Spain was Leah Manning, by now released from the pressures of her Labour candidacy in Sunderland. When the war broke out, Manning went at once to Madrid to help with the organisation of food and medical supplies. On returning to England she became secretary of the Aid Spain Committee, and then served as secretary of the Spanish Medical Aid Committee. Her frequent visits to Spain took her into the danger zones, and she was near Guernica, the Basque capital, when it was savagely bombed by the

Leah Manning: permission to carry arms, Bilbao, 1937. Photo: Victor Gollancz

Nazis. Under siege at Bilbao in May 1937, Manning arranged for the evacuation of Basque children and, following a hurried flight to London, she virtually bludgeoned an unwilling Home Secretary into allowing the children to enter England.

Some 20–30 refugee children from the Basque country were housed at Tynemouth by the local trades council. The ILP was one of the groups active in raising money for the children and represented on the management committee of the residential home created for the refugees. A smaller home was also opened at Hexham, but suffered from lack of local support. Throughout the country, about four thousand Basque children were sheltered by political, trade union, Co-operative and religious organisations, despite the frantic efforts of the Londonderrys and the *Daily Mail* to quickly hand the refugees over to Franco.

Another figure connected with the refugee children was the Tynesider Isabel Brown. Born into poverty, Isabel Brown had been active in first the Labour Party and then the Communist Party in Sunderland, South Shields and Boldon in the early 1920s. Her commitment took her to live in other parts of the country but during the Spanish War she worked tirelessly, often with Ellen Wilkinson and Leah Manning, and visited Spain, providing material help and bringing back first-hand information.[55]

The *Linaria*

Anti-fascists who had faced down Mosley took a considerable part in the Spanish War. One example was Alec "Spike" Robson, a veteran of the anti-Blackshirt battles in North Shields. Fresh from beating racial discrimination practised by the employers on Shields merchant ships, as well as organising multi-racial demonstrations in Cape Town, South Africa, against Mussolini's invasion of Abyssinia, Robson made a piece of maritime history in February 1937. He had joined the crew of the *S.S. Linaria*, a North Shields cargo carrier, which had docked in Boston on the American East Coast to collect coal for a Black Sea port. The ship's agents then announced that the *Linaria* would carry nitrates to a Fascist-held port in Spain. Alec Robson recalled:

"We were told by the agents that the nitrates were to be used for fertiliser. The crew told the agents that the bodies of the women and children of Spain were the fertilisers and that nitrates would be used for explosives by Franco's fascists. The crew refused to sail and held a sit-down strike for three weeks."

Eventually, the British consul at Boston, hysterically waving a copy of Robson's Special Branch file supplied by Scotland Yard, had the *Linaria's* crew deported to Liverpool, where they faced 85 charges of breaching the Merchant Shipping Acts. All but one of the charges, impeding navigation, were gradually withdrawn in a highly political trial, and the crew were fined £2 each. Robson and the others appealed, won their point at the Liverpool Assizes, but then the employers took the case to the High Court. Defended by D.N. Pritt, a former Labour parliamentary candidate for Sunderland, the crew had the case dismissed and costs were awarded against the employers. It was a notable victory giving seafarers some protection under maritime law if they refused to sail into a war zone.[56]

The crew of the Linaria at Liverpool. Photo: North Mail & Newcastle Chronicle, 24 March 1937

International Brigades

With Spanish Fascism heavily reinforced by Nazi and Italian troops, and Western governments refusing to assist Spanish democracy, it fell to anti-fascists to offer military aid to the Republic. From 1936 this help included an International Brigade raised among anti-fascist volunteers from across the world, and other contingents allied with the various Spanish political movements. The North East of England rallied rapidly to the Cause, providing over a hundred men for Spain.

From the spring of 1937 the Independent Labour Party stationed a Tynesider, John McNair, in Barcelona to liaise with POUM, the left-wing Workers' Party of Marxist Unity. McNair had spent much of his early life living in poverty in North and South Shields. Through the struggle against hardship, he had gained a political education cemented by experiences as a five-shillings a week clerk with the Wallsend Slipway and Engineering Company prior to the First World War. At the same time, he had developed into a strong Socialist, actively involved with the ILP. Following a period working in France, he returned to England and started to organise ILP aid for the POUM. At Barcelona, McNair helped to build a fighting unit composed of ILP volunteers and sympathisers, including the writer George Orwell whose book, *Homage to Catalonia*, became a classic, if controversial, account of war and revolution.

However, the International Brigade, recruited by the Communist Party but including Labour Party members, provided the main body of volunteers for Spain. George Aitken, the CP's North East district secretary, was sent to Spain to act as a political adviser to the International Brigade, and to apply his First World War military experience. And the best account of the International Brigaders from the North East remains Frank Graham's *Battle of Jarama*. Frank Graham took part in the Brigade, having been an NUWM official in Sunderland and Teesside, as well as a Communist student organiser in London where he often confronted Mosley's Blackshirts.

Apparently, the first to leave for Spain "in the Christmas of 1936 were four young men" from Sunderland. These included nineteen-years old Edgar Wilkinson, who had taken part in the 1936 Hunger March to London, and Thomas Dolan, a 6' tall, stoical anti-fascist who, like Frank Graham, had been active in the fight against the Blackshirts. Both Wilkinson and Dolan were killed defending Madrid from the Fascists.

Others followed from Sunderland. Bobbie Mackie and Ernest Lower, travelling secretly by sea to evade border controls, were torpedoed by an Italian submarine. Lower was drowned but Mackie swam ashore, crossed the Pyrennes at night and was fatally wounded serving with the International Brigade at Brunete in July 1937. The Sunderland group soon increased in size. Mick Morgan, E. Gibson, Harry Madden, B. Summers, B. McQuade, William Parlett and Bobbie Quaile joined in 1937. Quaile came from Hylton and had been an athlete and a weight-lifting champion. He was twice wounded in Spain.

Further volunteers were drawn from Newcastle, Wallsend, Consett, Blaydon, South Shields and Blyth. One of these was Bob Elliott, a Communist town councillor at Blyth, who had helped collect materials for a Tyneside food ship intended for Madrid. He had been prominent in the Hunger Marches and was a national leader of the National Unemployed Workers' Movement. Elliott gave his life at Villaneueva de la Canada on 6 July 1937, together with Bill Meredith, a company commander and Labour Party member from Bellingham in Northumberland. Wilf Jobling, a former national leader of the NUWM, employed in the housing department of Blaydon council and secretary of the local CP branch, was also killed at Madrid in March 1937 just six weeks after leaving England. Blaydon miner, Cliff Lawther, brother of the Durham miners' leader Will Lawther and Emmie Lawther's brother-in-law, died at Jarama, his last letter home urging greater efforts to combat Fascism: "We're doing our best here" the message ended.

Photos courtesy of Frank Graham. Wilf Jobling is pictured above (top right).

Spain volunteers return. Pictured at Central Station, Newcastle. The seven volunteers were Peter Donkin, John Corby, John Ritchards, who was wounded, Arthur Johnson, Sam Langley, who was wounded, Joe Blair and Dick Hearn. They are seen talking to Frank Graham on right. Photo: Frank Graham

Altogether, twenty-four of the North East volunteers were killed in Spain, including Frank Airlie, William Hudson, W. Johnson, S.E. Walsh and Harry Reynolds from Newcastle, Thomas Bromley (Southwick), S. Codling and J. Palzeard (South Shields), Robert Coutts (North Shields), Harry Smith and Frank Kerry (Gateshead), A. Leonard Robinson (Blackhall), Andrew Thompson (Durham), and Edward and William Tattam (Whitburn).[57]

But the Spanish Republic was sabotaged by the British and other governments who still preferred to appease the Nazis, and the Spanish people were sacrificed to decades of Fascist oppression. The surviving International Brigaders returned to England, receiving heroes' welcomes at Newcastle City Hall and Sunderland, and prepared for the next phase.

12 : A KNOCK ON THE DOOR

It was 3 June 1940. The Anglo-French military evacuation of Dunkirk was nearing completion. With invasion expected at any moment, rumours of enemy parachute landings abounded. Hitler's bombers had already attacked Middlesbrough on 24 May, making it the first English industrial town to suffer an air raid in this Second World War. And as tension mounted, the remaining Blackshirts in the North East heard a sharp knock on their doors.

Acting under Defence Regulation 18B, the Newcastle, Durham and Northumberland police swooped on several known Fascists. Mosley and the national leaders of the BUF had been rounded up during the previous week, and now it was the turn of the small fry. A pathetic sight was uncovered. Although Mosley's newspaper *Action* had claimed in November 1939 that Fascist activity was developing in the North East, and that Mosley had visited the area for "private talks" to encourage the membership, the real position was well removed from the bravado.

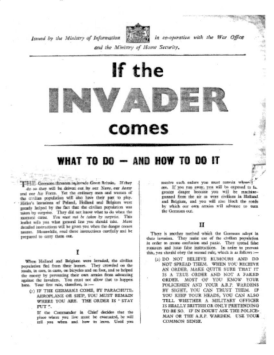

Chief Constable Crawley's secret reports to the Home Office in April 1940 noted that the BUF was active "but not much." By late May, the Newcastle public was freely offering information "concerning the British Union and its members." Then, on 3 June, Crawley arrested Colin Ferry, "the leader of the Union here", recovering documents, a flag and Fascist armlets from his home. A file on Ferry's political interests was forwarded to MI5. Wilfred Nicholson was also arrested and a Blackshirt uniform and membership subscription book was found.

The other Newcastle Fascist detained on 3 June was Margaret Camfield who, like Ferry and Nicholson, was in her early twenties. She had joined the BUF at Worthing in 1934, moving to Newcastle in 1938 to work as a hairdresser for J.T. Parrish & Co. Camfield was the BUF women's organiser in the area but, seemingly, "only about two women members" were enrolled. She had attended "two or three British Union public meetings in Newcastle" and admitted, under Special Branch questioning, that Fascism in the city was "on a modest scale."

Another long-serving Fascist, F.H. Jebb, seemed to have gone on the run. He had attempted to start a BUF branch, complete with "bodyguard", at Wooler, Northumberland, in January 1934, and was soon writing for *Fascist Week*. By June 1940, the police were searching for Jebb at addresses in Hawthorne Gardens, Whitley Bay, and Walbottle Hall, Northumberland. At some point, Jebb was caught and then detained until January 1941 when he returned to Walbottle Hall. Margaret Camfield was also released in January 1941, and soon moved to Birmingham. Other BUF people lingered longer in prison. Harry Simpson, a Washington Blackshirt was not freed until October 1941, and James Cherry, described by the Special Branch as "violently anti-Jewish", was not returned to his Newcastle home until March 1942.

Under Suspicion

Crawley confidently reported to London in August 1940: "British Union activities have ceased entirely." But this was not the whole story. The Special Branch continued to monitor local Fascists. Arthur Canning, a former Newcastle bus worker "recently connected with the British Union", was under surveillance at the Walker Naval Yard in October 1940. And Jebb together with two other Fascists, Lovegreen and

Thomas, were monitored "associating together" in January 1941 after their release from detention. James Elliott, Mosley's former secretary also came to light again in this period. According to the police, whose information may not have been entirely accurate in this case, Elliott had married one of John Beckett's ex-wives and moved to Newcastle upon Tyne, where he managed a cinema. On joining the Army at Gateshead in February 1941, he was kept under "careful observation."

Meanwhile, the detention of Fascists continued. Rose Jolly, a Durham BUF member was imprisoned in January 1941, and an actor named Anthony Le Suer (formerly Cruttwell) was arrested in Newcastle in April 1942. Le Suer had been in the BUF, was openly pro-Nazi and said he had joined the Army simply to obtain military information.

Crawley also intended to arrest "two male British subjects" in the event of invasion in August 1941. The identity of these dangerous characters has remained shrouded in mystery, along with that of another key target. According to the minutes of the Police Security Officers' Committee, a Special Branch/MI5 group which met weekly at Newcastle's Market Street Police HQ throughout the war, the security services' plans to deal with an invasion were updated in a curious way in June 1941. The committee resolved, menacingly, that in the event of Nazi invasion: "The rich and influential 'peace at all costs with Hitler' man must be disposed of before he has time to do damage." Who was this "rich and influential" figure against whom such drastic measures were to be taken? Was it Londonderry? It is difficult to see who else fitted the description in the North East. Despite spending much of the war in Ulster, Londonderry kept in touch with his Durham interests, and still held the high status of Lord Lieutenant of County Durham. The question is more easily posed than answered. Over half a century later, the evidence implicating "rich and influential" Nazi sympathisers and Mosleyites is still kept from public view (assuming that it has not been destroyed).[58]

*   *   *

The few Newcastle Fascists were dedicated, though they made little impact. Geoff Rossman, a teenage anti-fascist in the late-1930s, recalled the Newcastle Blackshirts smashing bookshop windows and assaulting people behind the Palace Cinema near the city's Pilgrim Street. Yet overall, the BUF had withered. John Beckett announced in January 1937 that an R. Sheville, a building contractor, boxer and BUF member since 1933, would stand as a Fascist candidate for Newcastle West at the next general election. The scheme came to nothing, not least because Beckett, fed up with Mosley's shortcomings, stormed out of the BUF in April 1937. Along with several prominent Fascists, including William Joyce, Vincent Collier and S.C. Crossley, Beckett formed a Nazi "National Socialist League". For Collier, the split may have been a merciful release. The decline of British Fascism had caused him acute embarrassment, as at Morpeth in January 1936 when only two people turned out for a well advertised public meeting. Collier believed Morpeth was "the worst meeting they had ever had." Two months later, the *Blackshirt* was reduced to appealing for news from Newcastle.[59]

Anti-fascism, contrastingly, was fairly vibrant. The Spanish War, of course, provided a principal focus. At the same time, a Northern Council Against Fascism circulated information and a news sheet among labour organisations on the Tyne and the Wear from 1936. Newcastle's People's Theatre produced anti-fascist plays such as *Professor Bernhardi*, an exposure of Viennese anti-semitism, in 1937, and a Left Theatre Group performed a similar function at a variety of

Anti-fascists at play: the Newcastle Young Communist League on a day trip to Seaburn c.1937–38. Photo courtesy of Dave Atkinson who is pictured on the left side, third from left in the second row

Anti-fascist demonstration moving along Crow Hall Lane, Felling, (above) to an open field, (below) c.1937. One of the banners depicts an International Brigader, W. Young, who 'Died in Defence of Democracy'. Photo: Jim Ancrum Collection

venues. Geoff Rossman recalled, too, that a "loose grouping" of anti-fascists embracing school students, businessmen, doctors, Communists and the occasional deputy head teacher, was busy in the 1937–39 period. And if the Fascists were less evident, there was no shortage of related issues. The South Shields police, for example, were still processing Austrian Jewish refugees, fleeing death threats, for deportation in July 1938.

This was a period in which some people took great risks with their lives, and not least Charlie Woods, the CP's Tyneside district secretary. During the late-1930s, Charlie Woods made undercover trips to Berlin as an agent of the Communist International, delivering messages and money to the German anti-Nazi resistance. On one occasion he had to run for his life down a Berlin backstreet because he could not bring himself to join in a public display of Nazi salutes. Charlie Woods was not the only Tynesider who made clandestine trips to meet German anti-fascists, and over half-a-century later some of those involved remain reluctant to reveal details of their experiences.[60]

Cable Street

Nationally, the BUF had been reduced, by a combination of hard opposition and a self-acquired disreputable image, to a largely London-based movement after 1934–35. Mainly for this reason, Mosley concentrated his forces on a "conquest of the streets" in the capital. Mussolini and Hitler had used this tactic, and Mosley thought he could repeat their success by marching through London's East End. Over the summer of 1936, as the *Tribune* journalist Frederic Mullally explained in his book *Fascism Inside England*, the Mosleyites held marches through the East End, whipping up hatred against the Jews. Protected by large forces of police, the Blackshirts' "display of strength and arrogance" attracted "hundreds of East London youths" who "flocked to the recruiting officers, hurriedly donned the black shirt, and joined the local Blackshirt gangs which made fascist sport" of the Jewish community.

Encouraged by this initial triumph, Mosley prepared for a great demonstration on 4 October 1936 – the fourth anniversary of the birth of the BUF. A mass rally was planned at Tower Hill as a prelude to four separate marches through the East End to meetings which Mosley would address in turn. Despite calls to ban the marches from all of East London's mayors, the Home Secretary and the Commissioner of Metropolitan Police deployed thousands of foot and mounted police to safeguard the Fascists' routes. As 7000 Blackshirts prepared to march, the police tried to clear their path. Neither party had reckoned on the determination of anti-fascists and the Jewish population to stand their ground. Utilising the Spanish rallying cry "They Shall Not Pass!", 10,000 ex-servicemen blocked the main Fascist route, forcing the police to move towards Cable Street.

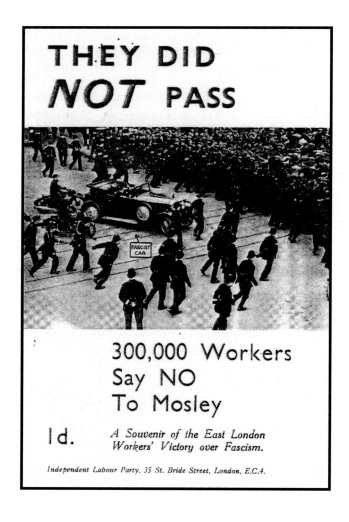

At Cable Street, the police found hostile crowds of 50,000. Mullally wrote that the anti-fascists had constructed "a huge barricade, hastily built with paving stones, hoardings, timber raided from a builder's yard and an overturned lorry." The roadway leading to the barricade was "strewn with broken glass as a defence against mounted police." More than a dozen baton charges were made by hundreds of police before the barricade was breached, but the resistance was not broken. The anti-fascists simply "regrouped in their thousands and prepared new barricades behind the first." Unable to disperse the anti-fascists, the Commissioner told Mosley (who had bought a new uniform for the occasion) that it was all over and ordered him to stay away from the East End. Emulating on a greater scale the Tyneside successes of 13 and 14 May 1934, the Battle of Cable Street was a historic victory for anti-fascism in England.

The following year, October 1937, Mosley targetted South London. This march, in Mullally's words, "ended in some of the worst street fighting the capital has seen [as] terrified householders found their quiet Sunday afternoon streets turned into battlefields, their doorsteps into dressing stations, manned by St. John's Ambulance men … Mounted and foot police, with lashing batons, swept again and again into the crowds of anti-fascist demonstrators … side-streets were strewn with the injured, many of them women, struck down in these charges, and more than 100 anti-fascists were arrested." But the point was made, and the Blackshirts were never again able to mount a large, provocative march through the streets of any British city.

Terms Of Defeat

It would be wrong to conclude that Fascism was completely defeated as a result of losing dramatic street confrontations. Fascism certainly did not disappear on the Tyne and the Wear after May 1934. And Frederic Mullally noted that in the eight months following Cable Street "BUF violence in the East End reached new depths of savagery as the movement fought to regain the prestige lost in October 1936." Individual acts of violence against Jews got worse after Cable Street. Organised Fascism continued to function. David Lewis, in a detailed study of the BUF, *Illusions of Grandeur*, found that the Fascists held 2108 meetings in East London between 1936–38, and regularly managed to disrupt meetings arranged by the Labour, Liberal, and Tory parties as well as church and Co-operative events.[61]

The importance of the Tyneside and London trials of strength really rested in two things. Firstly, anti-fascism engaged substantial numbers of people. Stopping Fascism came to be seen as a widespread responsibility, and the organising methods enabled large-scale participation. This contributed to changing the political atmosphere and thereby isolating Fascism. In this respect, anti-fascism was far more effective than government bans on wearing uniforms and holding marches imposed under the 1936 Public Order Act (Chief Constable Crawley rightly advised the Home Office that prohibiting Fascist uniforms would not get to the root of the problem).

Secondly, the BUF was denied its "conquest of the streets". For Mosley, the consequence was double-edged. On the one hand, the demoralised BUF was engulfed by splits, particularly on Tyneside and then nationally. And failure also undermined the utility of Fascism. Mosley's wealthy, closet sympathisers were unlikely to waste their time on a collection of losers. Locked into a downward spiral, the Fascists sustained themselves by growing more vicious, yet it was a viciousness born of defeat.

13 : AFTERMATH

The outbreak of war in September 1939 signalled the end of the Blackshirts, but not of Mosley. His internment was revoked in November 1943. The Newcastle police reported to the Home Office that public opinion was "surprised and dismayed somewhat" by Mosley's release, and that protest meetings had taken place. A broadsheet, *The People Against Mosley*, was widely circulated by the CP's North East district committee, prompting petitions calling for Mosley to be put on trial. With a touch of irony, the CP's Newcastle address was now 2 Clayton Street, which had been the Blackshirt headquarters in 1934.

AN ANTI-FASCIST BROADSHEET
Issued by the NORTH-EAST DISTRICT COMMITTEE OF THE COMMUNIST PARTY.

PUT
MOSLEY
BACK IN GAOL

PRICE 1D

3 DEC 1943

The people are in a white heat of anger at the news of Mosley's release.

Anti-fascist broadsheet bearing the Newcastle Chief Constable's official stamp!

Mosley, neatly escaping the wreckage that Fascism made of other people's lives, resided comfortably in England and France until his death in 1980. His several abortive Fascist revivals were marked by an increasingly squalid descent into racial hatred. At his first attempt in 1948–49 he was joined by some old faithfuls, briefly including Tommy Moran who, with his wife, was still rabidly anti-semitic.

Moran had gone through rough-houses and prisons for "the Leader" over fifteen years, only to discover that he was no longer wanted. Mosley preferred new faces. "Bitterly disillusioned", Moran's connection with Mosley finally ended in a ragged, angry East London street scene in February 1949. To the amusement of hovering anti-fascists, Moran

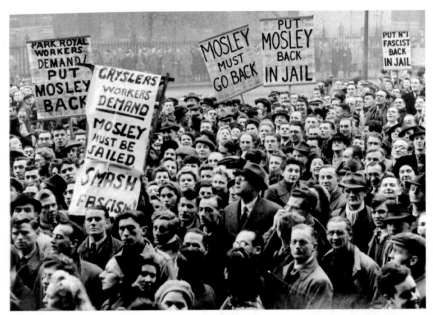

'Put Mosley Back In Jail': Representatives of 20,000 industrial workers lobby the House of Commons, 23 November 1943. Photo: Newcastle Chronicle & Journal

revealed to a small open air meeting that Mosley's "conception of leadership" was "dictatorship" and his "idea of service" was "slavery". For a self-styled intellectual, Moran was a remarkably slow learner. Nevertheless, he did learn and ended his days as an anti-fascist.

Alec Miles also saw the error of his ways, if sooner than Moran. According to Len Edmondson, Alec Miles wrote a condemnation of the BUF that may have been published under the London-based Tyneside writer Jack Common's name in the late-1930s. Miles went to sea to escape Blackshirt retribution, but was living back on Tyneside in the early 1950s.

Some of the other actors in our drama had grim fortunes. William Joyce was hanged as a traitor at Wandsworth prison in 1946. His capture in North Germany was due partly to a sharp-eyed Geordie soldier, Jimmy Evans from Newcastle, who, spotting Joyce living near to the Danish border, promptly alerted the military authorities. Ribbentrop was also executed. His pleas to call Lord Londonderry as a character witness at his war crimes trial went unheeded.

John Beckett spent three and a half years in prisons from May 1940. Afterwards, he obtained patronage from the Duke of Bedford who had "radical" political ambitions, but Beckett's heart had gone out of politics. When the Duke died in 1953, Beckett scratched a living as best he could and embraced Catholicism. He died in London in 1964, aged seventy, and working nights as a security guard for Securicor.

Chief Constable Crawley finally fell foul of the Home Office, and was held responsible for the unauthorised disposal of two fire engines, petrol and other supplies in 1943. He resigned together with the Newcastle watch committee, and died at Hexham in 1966.

What The Anti-Fascists Did Next

Several anti-fascists lived long and productive lives. Ruth Dodds devoted considerable time to developing the Little Theatre in Gateshead (she had been one of its founders). In the post-war years, she moved from Labour Party activity into working closely with the Society of Friends at a national level. Emmie Lawther continued with her Labour campaigns, especially in fields of concern to women, and she regularly chaired International Women's Day meetings in the 1950s. Education and improved child care services were among her passionate interests and, in 1961, she was elected to the Durham County Council. She died in 1965, leaving her body to the Newcastle University Medical School for research.

Ellen Wilkinson and Leah Manning went on to be Members of the historic Labour Parliament elected to lay the foundations of a welfare state and full employment in 1945. Wilkinson, as Minister of Education, died of pneumonia in 1947. Leah Manning spent many years, after leaving Parliament in 1950, as a teacher and promoter of infant care and family planning. She died in 1977 aged ninety-one.

Councillor Albert Gompertz became a South Shields institution in his own right, leading the town's Labour Party to political dominence and introducing many necessary reforms. He died in 1968.

Albert Gompertz as Mayor of South Shields in the early 1950s. Photo: South Tyneside Metropolitan Borough Council

'Spike' Robson lived an eventful life. Denied work on merchant ships after the *Linaria* affair, Robson was suddenly in demand again when war broke out. He had seen service in the First World War, being twice decorated for bravery, and in 1939 he enlisted for work on mine sweepers and landing craft. By 1943 he was running arms and supplies for anti-fascist partisans in Yugoslavia, and parachuting into the country at night to make contact with partisan units and evacuate the wounded. After the war, 'Spike' became the first Communist to be elected to the National Executive of the Seamen's Union and did much to improve wages and conditions in the merchant marine. He died at North Shields in 1979.

Charlie Woods survived his underground exploits in Hitler's Germany and lived to a great age on Tyneside, always holding firm to his Communist beliefs. Isabel Brown's physical health suffered under the strain of anti-fascist work, especially during the Second World War. Like numerous anti-fascists, her war against the Nazis had been fought strenuously for years prior to 1939. After the war she continued to promote women's rights and was a convinced Communist well into her 'eighties.

Similarly, Tom Brown remained a life-long Anarchist, producing articles and pamphlets throughout the 1950s, and regularly appearing at North East labour history gatherings until his death in the 1970s. John McNair, the ILP's man in Barcelona, served as his party's national secretary, and returned to live at East Howdon, Wallsend, in the 1950s. At the age of 74, he took an MA degree at Newcastle University, writing an analysis of George Orwell's work. McNair died at North Shields in 1968, having seen one of his comrades-in-arms from the ILP's Spanish contingent, Ted Fletcher, become a prominent Newcastle city councillor and then a Labour MP for Darlington.

Len Edmondson was an engineering union official for many years and remains prominent in the Anti-Apartheid Movement as well as campaigning for gypsy rights. Dave Atkinson, the anti-fascist postman, has kept up a life-time's commitment to trade unionism, having been a pillar of the Newcastle upon Tyne Trades Union Council and the postal workers' union.

Geoff Rossman went on to join the "43 Group" that did much to monitor, confront and derail Mosley's post-war revival. Rossman became chairman of the Northumberland branch of the "43 Group" in 1948 and the organisation soon enrolled over 100 keen members. This was enough to squash a Mosleyite effort to recruit among white collar workers, students, teachers and civil servants in Newcastle and Northumberland. The Fascists' outdoor meetings were closed down and their anti-semitic literature incinerated. Geoff Rossman has lost none of his zeal for the Cause.

Frank Graham has performed an invaluable task as a publisher of North East history at accessible prices, also winning further recognition for the sacrifices of the International Brigade. Tom Callaghan fascinates countless readers with his detailed descriptions of growing up in Benwell and Newcastle between the wars. Richard Kelly, as the first director of BBC Radio Newcastle, established a landmark in the region's media, and is never far from controversy. Tom Hadaway ceaselessly adds to Geordie pride and culture through his many plays and witty public appearances.[62]

Of the many, many others who died before their stories could be recorded, or whose identities have been lost to memory, this little book represents an incomplete tribute. It is an acknowledgement of the women and men who refused to do as they were told. They were beset with "good advice" to leave well alone and just get on with their football, washing, scraping a living or going to the pictures. The important questions could be left safely in the hands of bigger and more experienced chaps. From political platforms, police stations and newspaper barons came the golden wisdom that if you ignored the Blackshirts then they would simply go away. But the persistence of Mosley's cohorts on the Tyne and the Wear, even when the odds were against them, showed clearly that turning a blind eye was not an option. Moreover, the fate elsewhere of democrats, trade unionists, Jews, Africans, Socialists, Liberals, entire countries – the list was vast – illustrated the extreme danger of leaving Fascism to its own devices. Anti-fascism was a response of the common people who, detecting the nightmare, took a fine stand for life and liberty. Fortunately for us all, they won through in the end.

REFERENCES

1 Gentleman with a Duster, **The Conservative Mind,** (Mills & Boon, London, 1924), pp. 76–77, 82.

2 *Fascist Bulletin,* 13 June, 26 September, 3, 31 October 1925, 13 February 1926; *Whitley Seaside Chronicle,* 3 October 1925; *Newcastle Weekly Chronicle,* 24, 31 October 1925; *Journal,* 22 October 1925, 4 May 1926; Colin Cross, **The Fascists in Britain,** (Barrie & Rockliff, London, 1961), p. 57; Frederic Mullally, **Fascism Inside Britain,** (Morris Books, London, 1946), pp. 19–21; Kenneth Lunn, "The ideology and impact of the British Fascists in the 1920s" in Tony Kushner and Kenneth Lunn, **Traditions of intolerance: Historical perspectives on fascism and race discourse in Britain,** (Manchester University Press, Manchester, 1989).

3 *North Mail,* 17 May 1933; *For Stuart Barr see:* Dudley Grey interview (8 February 1977) in North Tyneside Community Development Project papers (T.W.A.S. 948/41); Tom Brown papers (in possession of Dr. Raymond Challinor); Len Edmondson interview, 17 June 1993; F.W. Manders, **A History of Gateshead,** (Gateshead Corporation, 1973), pp. 182–183; *For BUF origins see: Gateshead Herald,* March 1931; *Sunderland Echo,* 22 July 1931; D.S. Lewis, **Illusions of Grandeur: Mosley, Fascism and British Society, 1931–81,** (Manchester University Press, Manchester, 1987); for a statement of the BUF outlook see: James Drennan, **B.U.F. Oswald Mosley and British Fascism,** (Murray, London, 1934) … . Drennan was really W.E.D. (Bill) Allen, a former Tory MP, who was involved at the highest levels of the BUF whilst serving as an MI5 informer on the movement!

4 *North Mail,* 5 March, 16, 19 June 1933; *Journal,* 30 August 1933; *Fascist Week,* 9–15 March 1934; *Blackshirt,* 1 April 1934, 1 June 1934; *Sunderland Echo,* 17 March 1933.

5 Len Edmondson in Sharon Ferguson, **Labour Politics 1935–45: A Case Study of Koni Zilliacus and the Gateshead Labour Party and Trades Council,** (unpublishd mss at Gateshead Public Library, September 1988), pp. 29–30; *Fascist Week,* 1–7 December 1933; *The Northerner,* 1934; *Sunderland Echo,* 17, 31 March 1933, 2 February 1934; *Journal,* 29 May, 30 August 1933, 25 January 1934; *Newcastle Weekly Chronicle,* 3 February 1934; *Gateshead Herald,* September 1933; *North Mail,* 5, 8, 12, 29 May 1933; *New Leader,* 13 January, 3 February, 24 March, 14, 28 April, 3 November 1933.

6 *North Mail,* 26 June 1933; *Newcastle Weekly Chronicle,* 23 September, 16 December 1933; *Journal,* 3 August, 25 September 1933; *Sunderland Echo,* 4 November 1933, 26 January 1934; *Shields News,* 9 October, 1 November 1933; *Fascist Week,* 15–21 December 1933; *Blackshirt,* 24 August 1934; Transport & General Workers' Union, Area Committee, *Minutes,* 30 January 1934, (T.W.A.S. 673/2); Len Edmondson interview 17 June 1993; Labour Party Fascist Questionnaire, June 1934, LP/FAS/34/43.ii (Newcastle DLP) and LP/FAS/34/31.ii (Gateshead LP&TC); The BUF nationally received £40,000 from Mussolini in 1933–34 according to Richard Thurlow, 'The Secret History of British Fascism' in T. Kushner and

K. Lunn, **Traditions of Intolerance**, op.cit., p. 178; *New Leader*, 6 October, 17 November 1933.

7   Tom Hadaway letter to the author, 24 July 1993.

8   *Journal*, 1 February 1934; see also Richard Griffiths, **Fellow Travellers of the Right: British Enthusiasts for Nazi Germany, 1933–39,** (Constable, London, 1980), p. 50; *Fascist Week*, 9–15 February 1934; *Journal*, 3, 8 February 1934.

10 *North Mail*, 19 October 1934; *Gateshead Herald*, January 1934.

11 *Journal*, 28 February 1934; Richard Kelly/BBC Radio Newcastle script on "Italians in the North East" exhibition; Chief Constable A.E. Edwards (Middlesbrough) to Chief Constable F.J. Crawley (Newcastle upon Tyne), 11 June 1940 (T.W.A.S. T136/132); Peter and Leni Gillman, **"Collar the Lot!" How Britain Interned and Expelled its Wartime Refugees**, (Quartet Books, London, 1980), esp. Chapter 14 for connections between Italian community and Fascism; Nigel Todd, **The Militant Democracy: Joseph Cowen and Victorian Radicalism**, (Bewick Press, Whitley Bay, 1991) esp. pp 20–22 for historical background to Italian links with the North East.

12 *Journal* 3 June, 27 September 1933, 27 May 1936; David Nicholl, **The Golden Wheel: The Story of Rotary 1905 to the Present**, (Macdonald & Evans, Plymouth, 1984), esp. Chapter 18; Newcastle Rotary Club papers (T.W.A.S., 165/1/32); *Newcastle Weekly Chronicle*, 16 June 1934.

13 *Chester-le-Street Chronicle*, 24 November 1933; *Journal*, 1 June, 7 September 1934, 14 May 1936; *Newcastle Weekly Chronicle*, 16 June 1934. Labour Party Fascist Questionnaire, June 1934, LP/FAS/34/32.ii (Durham DLP).

14 *North Mail*, 27 July 1934; *Sunderland Echo*, 1 November 1933; *Journal*, 17 May 1934; G. Hetherington, **Portrait of a Company: Thermal Syndicate Limited 1906–1981**, (Thermal Syndicate Limited, Wallsend, 1981), esp. pp. 14, 115–116, 127–132; F. Brockway and F. Mullally, **Death Pays A Dividend**, (Gollancz, London, 1944), pp. 111–112; Bob Edwards, **War on the People: An Exposure of the Chemical Kings and their Nazi Associates**, (Independent Labour Party, London, 1943); for international business links with the Nazis see Charles Higham, **Trading With The Enemy**, (Robert Hale, London, 1983).

15 *Newcastle Weekly Chronicle*, 4 February 1933.

16 Tom Pickard, **Jarrow March**, (Allison & Busby, London, 1982), pp 26–28. Simon Haxey, **Tory M.P.**, (Gollancz, London, 1939), pp 231–232.

17 *Journal*, 6 February 1936; *North Mail*, 25 October 1934; Simon Haxey, **Tory M.P.**, op.cit., for Londonderry references; Anne de Courcey, **Circe: The Life of Edith, Marchioness of Londonderry**, (Sinclair-Stevenson, London, 1992) contains details of Nazi contacts; H. Montgomery Hyde, **The Londonderrys: A Family Portrait**, (Hamish Hamilton, London, 1979) offers useful background but glosses over the Nazi dimension.

18 *North Mail*, 1 February 1937; *Journal*, 22 February 1936.

19 Anne de Courcey, **Circe**, op.cit., pp. 272–277; *Journal*, 30 May 1936.

20 Michael Bloch, **Ribbentrop**, (Banton Press, New York, 1992), p. 113; Lord Londonderry, **Ourselves and Germany**, (Penguin Books, 1938), p. 119; Richard Griffiths, **Fellow Travellers**, op.cit., p. 218.

21 Simon Haxey, **Tory M.P.**, op.cit., esp. pp 201, 209, 220–221, 230.

22 Lord Londonderry, **Wings of Destiny**, (Macmillan, London, 1943), p. 209;
    Sharon Ferguson, **Labour Politics**, op.cit., p. 13; Colin Cross, **Fascists**,
    op.cit., p. 115; *North Mail*, 6 May 1938; *Journal*, 10 September 1934; *West
    London Press*, 25 November 1938; Haxey, **Tory M.P.**, op.cit., pp 215;
    Richard Griffiths, **Fellow Travellers**, op.cit., pp 262–263.
23 *Shields News*, 13 February 1934; *The Northerner*, 1934.
24 *Journal*, 1 June, 15,16,17 November 1934; *North Mail,*, 14 November 1934;
    Newcastle Weekly Chronicle, 27 July 1935.
25 Colin Cross, **The Fascists in Britain**, op.cit., pp 103–106; *Journal*, 5 March, 1,
    10, 14 May 1934; John D. Brewer, 'The BUF: Some Tentative Conclusions
    on its Membership' in S.U. Larsen (ed), **Who Were The Fascists?**, (Uni-
    versitetsforlaget, Bergen, 1980), p. 545; Colin Holmes, 'John Beckett' in
    Joyce Bellamy and John Saville (eds), **Dictionary of Labour Biography**, Vol.
    VI, (Macmillan, London, 1982), pp 24–29; see Francis Beckett, 'The Rebel
    Who Lost His Cause' in *History Today*, Vol. 44(5), May 1994, pp 36–42, for a
    valuable insight into Beckett's path to Fascism (Francis Beckett is also
    planning a full-length biography of his father, John).
26 *Shields News*, 30 April, 12 July 1934; *Journal*, 7 February, 5, 19 March, 9, 16,
    30 April, 14 May 1934; *Fascist Week*, 11–17 April, 11–17 May 1934;
    Sunderland Echo, 6, 23 February 1934; for Fenwick Whitfield, George
    Bestford and Terence Monaghan, see Keith Armstrong and Huw Beynon,
    **Hello, Are You Working? Memories of the Thirties in the North East of
    England**, (Strong Words, Whitley Bay, 1977), pp 15, 63, 83; Tom Callaghan,
    A Lang Way to the Panshop, (Frank Graham, Newcastle upon Tyne, nd), p.
    68; Tom Callaghan, Letter to the author, 5 July 1993; John Beckett, **After
    My Fashion (Twenty Post War Years)**, unpublished autobiography, 1939, p.
    355.
27 Interviews with Frank Graham (24 May 1993) and Len Edmondson (17
    June 1993), and Len Edmondson in Sharon Ferguson, **Labour Politics**,
    op.cit., p. 30; Len Edmondson, 'The Struggle Against Fascism in the
    Thirties' in North East Labour History *Bulletin*, No. 18, 1984; **The
    Newcastle upon Tyne and District Trades Council, 1873–1973: A Centenary
    History**, (Frank Graham, Newcastle upon Tyne, 1973), p. 35; Labour Party
    Fascist Questionnaire, LP/FAS/34/202, 22 June 1934 (Newcastle upon
    Tyne City Labour Party), and LP/FAS/34/300 (Jarrow Labour Party);
    Richard Croucher, **We Refuse To Starve In Silence: A History of the
    National Unemployed Workers' Movement 1920–46**, (Lawrence & Wishart,
    London, 1987), pp 187, 208; South Shields Labour Party and Trades
    Council, *Minutes*, 16 February, 1934
28 *Shields News*, 2, 5 February 1934; for Hilda Ashby and Connie Lewcock, see
    Keith Armstrong and Huw Beynon, **Hello, Are You Working?**, op.cit., pp
    44–45, 49; *Journal*, 16 April 1934; Ellen Wilkinson and Edward Conze, **Why
    Fascism?** (Selwyn & Blount, London, 1934); T.N. Shane, 'Ellen Wilkinson'
    in Herbert Tracey (ed), **The British Labour Party: Its History, Growth,
    Policy and Leaders**, Vol. III, (Caxton Publishing Company, London, 1948),
    pp 242–246; Betty Vernon, **Ellen Wilkinson 1891–1947**, (Croom Helm,
    London, 1982); Kenneth O. Morgan, 'Ellen Wilkinson' in **Labour People**,
    (Oxford University Press, 1987), pp 101–106; for Socialist League see:

Gateshead Herald, March, May, July 1934, March 1935; Tyneside Socialist League Executive *Minutes*, 1932–36, (Ruth Dodds Collection, Gateshead Central Library); Ben Pimlott, **Labour and the Left in the 1930s**, (Cambridge University Press, 1977); *New Leader*, 24 May 1935; Leah Manning, **A Life for Education: An Autobiography**, (Gollancz, London, 1970), esp. pp 102–105; Maureen Callcott and Barbara Nield, 'Leah Manning' in Joyce Bellamy and John Saville (eds), **Dictionary of Labour Biography, Vol. VII**, (Macmillan, London, 1984), pp 166–173; Ron Bill and Stan Newens, **Leah Manning**, (Leah Manning Trust/Square One Books, Harlow, 1991), pp 35–48; Steve Lawther, **Emmie Lawther: A Tribute**, (privately published, September, 1965); *New Leader*, 5 January 1934; Francis Beckett, 'The Rebel Who Lost His Cause', op.cit., p. 41; interview with Irene McManus, 7 February 1994.

29 *Journal*, 12 May 1934; Tom Brown in 'The Struggle Against Fascism in the Thirties' in North East Labour History *Bulletin*, No. 18, 1984; Albert Meltzer, **The Anarchists in London 1935–1955**, (Cienfuegos Press, Sanday, 1976), p. 16; 'Tyneside Fights the Fascists' in **Tyneside May Day 1992,** (Tyneside May Day Committee, Newcastle upon Tyne, 1992), pp 4–6.

30 *Journal*, 9, 28, 29 May 1934.

31 *Journal*, 2 May 1934; Tom Brown in North East Labour History *Bulletin*, op.cit; Len Edmondson interview, 17 June 1993.

32 *North Mail*, 14 May 1934; *Journal*, 14, 15, 17 May 1934; *News Chronicle*, 15 May 1934; Colin Cross, **The Fascists**, op.cit., p. 107; John Beckett, **After My Fasion**, op.cit., p. 358; *Daily Herald*, 29 May 1934.

33 *Journal*, 28 May, 1 June, 28 July 1934; *Fascist Week*, 25–31 May 1934. *Shields News*, 3 May 1934; Henry Maitles, 'Blackshirts across the border' in *Socialist Review*, February 1994, p. 23.

34 *Journal*, 1, 2 May 1934; *Manchester Guardian*, 17 May 1934; R. Ogle to Home Office, 15 May 1934 (PRO HO 144/20140–76); F.J. Crawley to Home Office, 15 May 1934 (PRO HO 144/20140–87 & 96); D.S. Lewis, **Illusions**, op.cit., p. 168; Stuart Rawnsley, 'The Membership of the BUF' in K. Lunn and Richard Thurlow (eds), **British Fascism**, (Croom Helm, London, 1980), p. 163; interview with Dave Atkinson, 20 June 1994.

35 *Fascist Week*, 25–31 May 1934; Dave Atkinson interview 23 June 1993; A.K. Chesterton, **Oswald Mosley,** (Action Press, London, 1937), pp 123/124; Tom Brown and Len Edmondson in North East Labour History *Bulletin*, op.cit; 'Tyneside Fights the Fascists', op.cit., pp 5–6. John Beckett, **After My Fashion**, op.cit., pp 355, 358.

36 Report on the Fascist Movement in the United Kingdom 18 June 1934, PRO HO 144/20141–293; The Fascist Movement in the United Kingdom: Report No. II: Developments during June and July 1934, (PRO HO 144/ 20142–108; Kell to Crawley, 9 June 1934, (PRO HO 144/20141- 352); for a detailed study of MI5 interest in the BUF see: Richard C. Thurlow, 'British Fascism and State Surveillance, 1934–45' in *Intelligence and National Security*, Vol. 3, January 1988, No. 1, pp 77–99.

37 Crawley to Kell, 12 June 1934 (PRO HO 144/20141–351); Newcastle *Evening Chronicle*, 11 January 1964; *Journal*, 29 January 1934, 6 October 1966; John Yearnshire, **Back on the Borough Beat: A Brief Illustrated**

History of the Sunderland Borough Police, (Yearnshire, Sunderland, 1987), pp 45, 53; Anthony Mason, The General Strike in the North East, (University of Hull Occasional Publication, No.3, 1970), pp 73–75; Nigel West, MI5: British Security Service Operations 1909–1945, (Triad/ Granada, London, 1983), pp 38–40; Christopher Andrew, Secret Service: The Making of the British Intelligence Community, (Heinemann, London, 1985), pp 59, 371–375; *York Free Press*, April/May-September 1978, nos. 24–26; *for further surveys of local BUF activities and Police reactions see:* S.M. Cullen, 'The British Union of Fascists, 1932–1940: ideology, membership and meetings', unpublished M.Litt thesis, University of Oxford, 1987.

38 *Blackshirt*, 8 June 1934; *North Mail*, 2, 4 June 1934; Len Edmondson interview, 17 June 1993.

39 *Journal*, 11, 25 June, 30 July 1934; *Newcastle Weekly Chronicle*, 23 June 1934; Newcastle upon Tyne Police *General Orders*, 27 July 1934 (T.W.A.S., T136/ 14); *North Mail*, 11, 22 June, 30 July 1934; *Daily Worker*, 21 June, 23 July 1934.

40 *Newcastle Weekly Chronicle*, 14 July 1934; *Shields News*, 4,5, 7, 10, 11, 12, 14 July 1934; *North Mail*, 26 July 1934; Tom Hadaway letter to author 24 July 1993; for Robson see (56) below.

41 PRO HO 144/20142, 144/20144 (123), 45/25385 (48); G.C. Webber, 'Patterns of Membership and Support for the British Union of Fascists' in *Journal of Contemporary History*, Vol. 19, No. 4, 1984.

42 *North Mail*, 16 August, 27 October, 14 November 1934; *Journal*, 15,16, 17 November 1934; *Blackshirt*, 23 November 1934; 'The Fascist Movement in the United Kingdom, Report No. VI: March 1935-October 1935' in PRO HO 45/25385 (48).

43 *Blackshirt*, 19 October, 16, 23 November 1934; *Journal*, 17 November 1934, 7 February 1936; Special Branch Report, 14 January 1935 in PRO HO 144/ 20144–197; Martin Durham, 'Gender and the BUF' in *Journal of Contemporary History*, Vol. 27, No. 3, July 1992.

44 Len Edmondson in North East Labour History *Bulletin*, No. 18, 1984; Len Edmondson interview, 17 June 1993; Hilda Ashby in Keith Armstrong and Huw Beynon, Hello, Are You Working?, op.cit., p. 44; *Journal*, 26 March, 27 May 1935; *Blackshirt*, 29 March 1935; *Comrade*, February/March 1990, p. 2; Colin Cross, The Fascists in Britain, op.cit., pp 145–146. *North Mail*, 16 July 1934.

45 D.S. Lewis, Illusions, op.cit., p. 122; *Daily Express*, 26 May 1935; *Blackshirt*, 31 May 1935; *Journal*, 6,14 June 1935; Crawley/Home Office corespondence, 28–29 May, 8 June 1935 in PRO HO 144/20144 (11), (18), (19).

46 *Journal*, 8,10 June 1935; *Blackshirt*, 14, 28 June, 26 July 1935; *Newcastle Weekly Chronicle*, 9 November 1935; Tom Callaghan, Those Were The Days, op.cit., p. 129/A Lang Way to the Panshop, op.cit., p. 67.

47 *Blackshirt*, 18 October 1935; Special Branch Report, 24 October 1935, in PRO HO 144/20145 (14); 'The Fascist Movement in the United Kingdom, Report No. V: Developments to the end of February 1935' in PRO HO/ 144/ 20144 (123); 'The Fascist Movement in the U.K., Report No. VI: March 1935-October 1935' in PRO HO 45/25385 (48).

48 Richard Kelly letter to the author, 28 July 1993; for Joyce see Francis
    Selwyn, **Hitler's Englishman: The Crime of Lord Haw-Haw**, (Penguin
    Books, London, 1993) and Rebecca West, **The Meaning of Treason**,
    (Macmillan, London, 1949); *Blackshirt*, 17 May 1935; *Sunderland Echo*, 10
    January 1934; *Journal*, 9, 10, 11 May 1935; *North Mail*, 12 December 1934;
    Shields Gazette, 10 May 1935.
49 See: PRO HO 45/25385–22.
50 George Hardy, **Those Stormy Years**, (Lawrence & Wishart, London, 1956),
    p. 225; John Charnley in Anon., **Mosley's Blackshirts: The Inside Story of
    the British Union of Fascists, 1932–40**, (Sanctuary Press, London, 1984), p.
    35; Len Edmondson interview, 17 June 1993; *Blackshirt*, 6 September 1935;
    Journal, 2 September, 2 October 1935.
51 *North Mail*, 10 May 1933; *Journal*, 23 March 1936; *Sunderland Echo*, 10 April
    1933; Tom Callaghan, **A Lang Way to the Panshop**, op.cit., p. 68; Lewis
    Olsover, **The Jewish Communities of North East England**, (Ashley Mark,
    Gateshead, 1981), pp 50–52; *Northern Echo*, 19 December 1933.
52 David Rosenberg, **Facing Up to Anti-Semitism: How the Jews in Britain
    Countered the Threats of the 1930s**, (JCARP, London, 1985), p. 16;
    Journal, 15 July 1935; *Newcastle Weekly Chronicle*, 27 July, 9 November 1935;
    David Clark, **We Do Not Want The Earth: The History of the South Shields
    Labour Party**, (Bewick Press, Whitley Bay, 1992), pp 74, 90–91; *Shieldsman*,
    22 March 1935.
53 Clark, **We Do Not Want The Earth**, ibid; *Shields Gazette*, 9 September, 28
    October 1935; *North Mail*, 22 June, 5 July 1934; South Shields Trades
    Council *Minutes*, 20 February 1934.
54 *Journal*, 9 September, 4 November 1935; *North Mail*, 29 May 1934, 4
    November 1935; *Blackshirt*, 18 October, 1, 8 November 1935; Barry Carr,
    'Black Geordies' in Robert Colls and Bill Lancaster, **Geordies: Roots of
    Regionalism**, (Edinburgh University Press, Edinburgh, 1992), pp 142–144.
55 Interviews with Len Edmondson (17 June 1993) and Dave Atkinson (23
    June 1993); Hilda Ashby in Keith Armstrong and Huw Beynon, **Hello, Are
    You Working?**, op.cit., p. 45; *North Mail*, 6 February 1937; *Journal*, 14 April
    1937; Northumberland and Tyneside Federation of Labour Parties,
    Minutes, September 1938; Noreen Branson, **History of the Communist
    Party of Great Britain, 1927–1941**, (Lawrence and Wishart, London, 1985),
    p. 225; David Bean, **Armstrong's Men: The Story of the Shop Stewards
    Movement in the Tyneside Works**, (Vickers Ltd., Newcastle upon Tyne,
    1967), p. 28; May Hill, **Red Roses for Isabel**, (May Hill, Preston, 1982), pp
    1–9, 81–83, 103; *New Leader*, 18 September, 1936; Jim Fyrth, **The Signal Was
    Spain: The Aid Spain Movement in Britain 1936–39**, (Lawrence and
    Wishart, London, 1986), pp 234, 272, 280–281; Leah Manning, **A Life for
    Education**, op.cit., Chapter X; Maureen Callcott and Barbara Nield, 'Leah
    Manning' in Bellamy and Saville, op.cit., pp 169–170.
56 *North Mail*, 15 January, 22 February 1937; John Corcoran (ed), **Spike: Alec
    'Spike' Robson 1895–1979: Class Fighter**, (North Tyneside Trades Union
    Council, North Shields, 1987), pp 7–12.
57 Peter Thwaites. 'The Independent Labour Party Contingent in the Spanish
    Civil War' in *Imperial War Museum Review* 1989, pp 50–61; Don Bateman,

John McNair's Spanish Diary, (Independent Labour Party, Manchester, n.d.) contains some material on McNair's early life and his own account of Spain; for more on McNair's friendship with Orwell see Mike Jamieson, 'Escape from Gunfire' in the Newcastle upon Tyne *Evening Chronicle,* 27 December 1983; there is a fine and detailed obituary of McNair in the *Wallsend Weekly News,* 23 February 1968, p. 9; Frank Graham, **Battle of Jarama 1937; The Story of the British Battalion of the International Brigade in Spain,** (Frank Graham, Newcastle upon Tyne, 1987), pp 72–76; see also Bill Alexander, **British Volunteers for Liberty: Spain 1936–39,** (Lawrence & Wishart, London, 1986 edn), esp. pp 39, 67, 74, 122, 243, 263–276; *North Mail,*12,18 March 1937; interview with Irene McManus, 7 February 1994; Richard Croucher, **We Refuse to Starve In Silence,** op.cit., p. 188.

58 *Journal,* 27 January 1934; *Fascist Week,* 25–31 May 1934; *Action,* 16 November 1939; *Newcastle Journal & North Mail,* 5 June 1940; Newcastle upon Tyne Police *Special Reports/Suspect Lists,* 25 April, 24 May, 30 May, 3 June, 7 June, 16 August 1940 (T.W.A.S. T136/131; 134; 137); Newcastle upon Tyne Police, *North Region Special Branch/Police Security Officers Minutes of Meetings,* 3 October 1940, 1 February, 1 March, 5/15 June, 15 October 1941, 15 March, 1 April 1942 (T.W.A.S. T136/127); Crawley to O/c Northumberland Division, 14 May 1941 (T.W.A.S. T136/132).

59 Geoff Rossman interview, 9 June 1993; *Action,* 7 November 1936, 23 January 1937; *Blackshirt,* 21 March 1936; *Journal,* 13 January 1936; Richard Griffiths, **Fellow Travellers,** op.cit., p. 278.

60 *Journal,* 5 April 1937; *North Mail,* 2 July 1938; interviews with Dave Atkinson (23 June 1993) and Geoff Rossman (9 June 1993); Charlie Woods information provided by Brian Topping.

61 Frederick Mullally, **Fascism,** op.cit., pp 70–75; Phil Piratin **Our Flag Stays Red,** (Lawrence & Wishart, London, 1978 edn), pp 15–33; Independent Labour Party, **They Did *Not* Pass: A Souvenir of the East London Workers' Victory over Fascism,** (ILP, London, 1936); D.S. Lewis, **Illusions,** op.cit., pp 123–128.

62 Len Edmondson interview (17 June 1993); Chief Constable Crawley to Home Office, 3 & 30 December 1943 (T.W.A.S. T136/134); John Corcoran (ed), **Spike … Alec 'Spike' Robson,** op.cit., pp 12/17; May Hill, **Red Roses,** op.cit; *Wallsend Weekly News,* 23 February 1968; *Reynolds News,* 6 February 1949; *Jewish Chronicle,* 11 February 1949; Morris Beckman, **The 43 Group: The Untold Story of their Fight Against Fascism,** (Centreprise Publications, London, 1993 edn), pp 121/122, 152/153, 180; Sid Chaplin, 'The Truth and Richard Kelly' in Sid Chaplin, **A Tree With Rosy Apples,** (Frank Graham, Newcastle upon Tyne, 1972), pp 118/123; Francis Beckett, 'The Rebel Who Lost His Cause' in *History Today,* Vol. 44(5), May 1994, p. 40; Steve Lawther, **Emmie Lawther,** op.cit., p. 12; Newcastle *Evening Chronicle,* 8 July 1993.

Note: T.W.A.S = Tyne & Wear Archives Service
       PRO = Public Records Office

INDEX

Members of Parliament
  Attlee, Clement 16, 36
  Baldwin, Stanley 29
  Bevan, Aneurin 19
  Castlereagh, Viscount 33
  Chamberlain, Neville 33
  Cripps, Stafford 19
  Denville, Alfred 33
  Eden, Anthony 33
  Grattan-Doyle, Nicholas 33
  Lawson, Jack 60
  MacDonald, Ramsay 7, 10, 12, 17, 29
  Magnay, Thomas 33
  Maxton, James 56
  Russell, Sir Alexander 33
Middlesbrough 22, 42, 88, 104
Mill Lane 69
Molloy, Barney 68
Monaghan, Terence 38, 90
Mond, Sir Alfred 36-37
Morpeth 107
Moscow 17, 18
Mosley, Lady 78
Mosley, Sir Oswald 7-10, 15, 20, 26, 33, 35, 38, 58, 60, 69-72, 79, 82, 104, 107, 109, 113, 117, *passim*
Mullally, Frederick 109-111
Mussolini, Benito 3, 6, 8, 22, 24, 26, 28, 33, 36, 85, 93, 96

National Council for Civil Liberties 3
National Government 3, 7, 29, 47, 69
National Unemployed Workers' Movement (NUWM) 14, 39, 73, 80, 97, 101
Nazis 9, 12, 18, 20, 23, 24, 29, 44, 53
  Bene, Otto 85, 86
  Berens, Dr. P. 88
  Hacker, Wilhelm 91
  Goering, Herman 30, 32
  Hitler, Adolf 3, 4, 10, 21, 24, 26, 27, 30, 31, 32, 82, 85, 96
  Neukirch, F.K. 21
  Ribbentrop, von 30-32, 114-115
  Schippert, Karl 24
  Telle, Dr. H.G. 88
New Party 8
Newspapers
  Action 104
  Adelphi 50-51
  Anglo-German Review 32, 33
  Berliner Tageblatt 32

Blackshirt 73, 75, 77, 80, 81, 82, 86, 91, 107
Comrade 79
Daily Express 80
Daily Herald 96
Daily Mail 15, 20, 26, 78, 98
Daily Worker 69, 70
Evening Chronicle 10, 68
Fascist Week 21, 38, 62, 105
Gateshead Herald 45, 46
Journal 26, 30, 34, 37, 38, 54, 55, 56, 69, 86
Newcastle Weekly Chronicle 26
News Chronicle 58
North Mail 57, 71, 75, 76, 94
Northern Echo 88, 89
Northerner 13, 14, 23
Patriot 5
Shields Gazette 94
Shieldsman 89
Shields News 48, 73
Sunderland Echo 37, 88
Times, The 33
Tribune 109
Newcastle upon Tyne *passim*
Nicholl, David Shelley 23
North Shields 1, 7, 8, 37, 39, 47, 71-73, 99, 100, 103, 116-117
Northumberland 5, 6, 18, 19, 39, 78, 101, 105, 117

Ogle, R. 60
Olympia 78
Orwell, George 100, 117

Pallister, James 61
Paris 13
Peckham 36
Police
  Cardiff 66
  Durham 104
  Gateshead 58, 60, 62, 68
  Manchester 66
  Metropolitan 66, 109-111
  Newcastle upon Tyne 35, 56, 60-67, 69-71, 80, 82-86, 101-102, 105-106, 113, 117
  Northumberland 104
  South Shields 90-91, 93, 109
  Sunderland 66
  York 66
Pritt, D.N. 47, 99
Public Order Act, 1936 3, 112